Communications
in Computer and Information Science 1656

More information about this series at https://link.springer.com/bookseries/7899

Stefano Marrone · Martina De Sanctis ·
Imre Kocsis · Rasmus Adler · Richard Hawkins ·
Philipp Schleiß · Stefano Marrone ·
Roberto Nardone · Francesco Flammini ·
Valeria Vittorini (Eds.)

Dependable Computing – EDCC 2022 Workshops

SERENE, DREAMS, AI4RAILS
Zaragoza, Spain, September 12, 2022
Proceedings

Editors

Stefano Marrone [iD]
University of Campania "Luigi Vanvitelli"
Caserta, Italy

Imre Kocsis [iD]
Budapest University of Technology
and Economics
Budapest, Hungary

Richard Hawkins [iD]
University of York
York, UK

Stefano Marrone [iD]
University of Naples Federico II
Naples, Italy

Francesco Flammini [iD]
Mälardalen University
Västerås, Sweden

Martina De Sanctis [iD]
Gran Sasso Science Institute
L'Aquila, Italy

Rasmus Adler [iD]
Fraunhofer Institute for Experimental
Software Engineering IESE
Kaiserslautern, Germany

Philipp Schleiß
Fraunhofer Institute for Cognitive Systems
IKS
Munich, Germany

Roberto Nardone [iD]
Parthenope University of Naples
Naples, Italy

Valeria Vittorini [iD]
University of Naples Federico II
Naples, Italy

ISSN 1865-0929   ISSN 1865-0937 (electronic)
Communications in Computer and Information Science
ISBN 978-3-031-16244-2   ISBN 978-3-031-16245-9 (eBook)
https://doi.org/10.1007/978-3-031-16245-9

This Springer imprint is published by the registered company Springer Nature Switzerland AG
The registered company address is: Gewerbestrasse 11, 6330 Cham, Switzerland

Preface

The European Dependable Computing Conference (EDCC) is an international annual forum for researchers and practitioners to present and discuss their latest research results on theory, techniques, systems, and tools for the design, validation, operation, and evaluation of dependable and secure computing systems.

Traditionally one-day workshops precede the main conference: the workshops complement the main conference by addressing dependability or security issues on specific application domains or by focusing in specialized topics, such as system resilience.

The 18th edition of EDCC was held in Zaragoza, Spain, during September 12–15, 2022. After two years of virtual events, due to the COVID-19 pandemic, EDCC 2022 returned as a physical event, allowing researchers and practitioners to meet and exchange ideas face to face.

The workshops day was held on Monday, September 12, 2022.

Four workshop proposals were submitted to this 18th edition and, after a thoughtful review process led by the workshop chair, all of them were accepted. The evaluation criteria for the workshops selection included the relevance to EDCC, the timeliness and expected interest in the proposed topics, the organizers' ability to lead a successful workshop, and their balance and synergy.

These joint proceedings include the accepted papers from three of these workshops:

- 14th International Workshop on Software Engineering for Resilient Systems (SERENE 2022);
- 3rd International Workshop on Dynamic Risk managEment for Autonomous Systems (DREAMS 2022);
- 3rd International Workshop on Artificial Intelligence for RAILwayS (AI4RAILS 2022).

All these three workshops together received a total of 22 submissions. Each workshop had an independent Program Committee, which was in charge of reviewing and selecting the papers submitted to the workshop. DREAMS 2022 and AI4RAILS 2022 adopted a single-blind review process while SERENE 2022 adopted a double-blind one. All the workshop papers received three reviews per paper (67 reviews in total). Out of the 22 submissions, 11 papers were selected to be presented at the workshops (acceptance rate of 50%) and all of these 11 papers were included in these proceedings.

Many people contributed to the success of the EDCC workshops day of this 18th edition. I would like to express my gratitude to all those supported this event. First, I thank all the workshops organizers for their dedication and commitment, the authors who contributed to this volume, the reviewers for their help in the paper assessment, and the workshops participants.

I would also like to thank all the members of the EDCC Steering and Organizing Committees, in particular Simona Bernardi and José Merseguer (the General Chairs), who worked hard to bring back EDCC as a physical event. A special thank you to Simin Nadjm-Tehrani (the Program Chair) for her precious suggestions and Diego Peréz Palacín and Francesco Flammini (the Publicity Chairs) for disseminating the calls for papers.

Finally, many thanks to the staff of Springer who provided professional support through all the phases that led to this volume.

September 2022   Stefano Marrone

Organization

EDCC Steering Committee

Karama Kanoun (Chair)	LAAS-CNRS, France
Jean-Charles Fabre	LAAS-CNRS, France
Felicita Di Giandomenico	ISTI-CNR, Italy
Johan Karlsson	Chalmers University of Technology, Sweden
Henrique Madeira	Universidade de Coimbra, Portugal
Miroslaw Malek	Università della Svizzera italiana, Switzerland
Juan Carlos Ruiz	Technical University of Valencia, Spain
Janusz Sosnowski	Warsaw University of Technology, Poland
Michael Paulitsch	Intel, Germany
Alexander Romanovsky	Newcastle University, UK

EDCC 2022 Organization

General Chairs

Simona Bernardi	University of Zaragoza, Spain
José Merseguer	University of Zaragoza, Spain

Program Chair

Simin Nadjm-Tehrani	Linköping University, Sweden

Web Chair

Elena Gómez-Martínez	Universidad Autónoma de Madrid, Spain

Local Organization Chairs

Pilar González	I3A, Spain
Jorge Júlvez	University of Zaragoza, Spain

Workshops Chair

Stefano Marrone	University of Campania "Luigi Vanvitelli", Italy

Students Forum Chair

Ibéria Medeiros   University of Lisbon, Portugal

Fast Abstracts Chair

Geert Deconinck   KU Leuven, Belgium

Industry Track Chair

Michael Paulitsch   Intel, Germany

Publication Chair

Matthias Eckhart   SBA Research and University of Vienna, Austria

Publicity Chairs

Diego Peréz Palacín   Linnaeus University, Sweden
Francesco Flammini   Mälardalen University, Sweden

Workshop Editors

Workshops Chair

Stefano Marrone
University of Campania "Luigi Vanvitelli", Italy
stefano.marrone@unicampania.it

SERENE

Martina De Sanctis
Gran Sasso Science Institute, Italy
martina.desanctis@gssi.it

Imre Kocsis
Budapest University of Technology and Economics, Hungary
kocsis.imre@vik.bme.hu

DREAMS

Rasmus Adler
Fraunhofer IESE, Germany
Rasmus.Adler@iese.fraunhofer.de

Richard Hawkins
University of York/Assuring Autonomy International Program, UK
richard.hawkins@york.ac.uk

Philipp Schleiß
Fraunhofer IKS, Germany
philipp.schleiss@iks.fraunhofer.de

AI4RAILS

Stefano Marrone
University of Naples Federico II, Italy
stefano.marrone@unina.it

Roberto Nardone
University Parthenope, Italy
roberto.nardone@uniparthenope.it

Francesco Flammini
Mälardalen University and Linnaeus University, Sweden
`francesco.flammini@mdh.se`

Valeria Vittorini
University of Naples Federico II, Italy
`valeria.vittorini@unina.it`

Contents

Workshop on Software Engineering for Resilient Systems (SERENE)

International Workshop on Software Engineering for Resilient Systems (SERENE)

Workshop Description

SERENE 2022 was the 14th International Workshop on Software Engineering for Resilient Systems, held as a satellite event of the European Dependable Computing Conference (EDCC).

Resilient systems withstand, recover from, and adapt to disruptive changes with acceptable degradation in their provided services. Resilience is particularly remarkable for modern software and software-controlled systems, many of which are required to continually adapt their architecture and parameters in response to evolving requirements, customer feedback, new business needs, platform upgrades, etc. Despite frequent changes and disruptions, the software is expected to function correctly and reliably. This is particularly important for software systems that provide services which are critical to society, e.g., in transportation, healthcare, energy production, and e-government. Since modern software should be developed to cope with changes, unforeseen failures, and malicious cyber-attacks efficiently, design for resilience is an increasingly important area of software engineering.

SERENE has a long tradition of bringing together leading researchers and practitioners, to advance the state of the art and to identify open challenges in the software engineering of resilient systems.

This year, 7 papers were submitted. Each submission was reviewed by three members of the Program Committee, and two papers were accepted for presentation.

We would like to thank the SERENE Steering Committee and the SERENE 2022 Program Committee, who made the workshop possible. We would also like to thank EDCC for hosting our workshop, the EDCC workshop chair Stefano Marrone for his help and support, and the editors of CCIS series at Springer who accepted the papers for publication. The logistics of our job as Program Chairs were facilitated by the EasyChair system.

Organization

General Chairs

Patrizio Pelliccione   Gran Sasso Science Institute, Italy
Zoltáán Micskei   Budapest University of Technology
     and Economics, Hungary

Steering Committee

Didier Buchs   University of Geneva, Switzerland
Henry Muccini   University of L'Aquila, Italy
Patrizio Pelliccione   Gran Sasso Science Institute, Italy
Alexander Romanovsky   Newcastle University, UK
Elena Troubitsyna   KTH Royal Institute of Technology, Sweden

Organizing Committee

Martina De Sanctis   Gran Sasso Science Institute, Italy
Imre Kocsis   Budapest University of Technology
     and Economics, Hungary

Program Committee

Marco Autili   University of L'Aquila, Italy
Georgios Bouloukakis   Télécom SudParis, France
Radu Calinescu   University of York, UK
Andrea Ceccarelli   University of Florence, Italy
Felicita Di Giandomenico   CNR-ISTI, Italy
Carlos Gavidia-Calderon   The Open University, UK
Nikolaos Georgantas   Inria, France
Simos Gerasimou   University of York, UK
Jérémie Guiochet   Université de Toulouse 3, LAAS-CNRS,
     France
Linas Laibinis   Vilnius University, Lithuania
Istvan Majzik   Budapest University of Technology
     and Economics, Hungary
Paolo Masci   National Institute of Aerospace, Langley
     Research Center, USA

Henry Muccini	University of L'Aquila, Italy
András Pataricza	Budapest University of Technology and Economics, Hungary
Cristina Seceleanu	Malardalen University, Sweden
Alin Stefanescu	University of Bucharest, Romania
Elena Troubitsyna	KTH Royal Institute of Technology, Sweden
Karthik Vaidhyanathan	University of L'Aquila, Italy
Marco Vieira	University of Coimbra, Portugal
Apostolos Zarras	University of Ioannina, Greece
Riccardo Pinciroli	Gran Sasso Science Institute, Italy

Web Chair

| Amleto Di Salle | University of L'Aquila, Italy |

AuditTrust: Blockchain-Based Audit Trail for Sharing Data in a Distributed Environment

Hugo Lloreda Sanchez[1] , Sophie Tysebaert[1] , Annanda Rath[2]([✉]) ,
and Etienne Rivière[1]([✉])

[1] EPL/ICTEAM, UCLouvain, Louvain-la-Neuve, Belgium
etienne.riviere@uclouvain.be
[2] Sirris, Brussels, Belgium
annanda.rath@sirris.be

Abstract. There has been a significant recent interest in trust-building technologies for decentralized environments, especially for sharing data between mutually distrusting entities. One of the critical challenges in this context is to ensure that shared data cannot be tampered with, and that access to this data can always be traced and audited in a secure and trustworthy way, e.g., by using an access log to detect tampering. However, for audit trail data to be useful, it must be correct, immutable, and tied with access control mechanisms. We present Audit-Trust, a blockchain-based secure audit trail for data sharing in a distributed environment. We prototype AuditTrust using several technologies, such as Hyperledger Besu, IPFS, the Intel SGX TEE, and Vault. Our evaluation of AuditTrust examines the latency costs of auditing and access control and shows the effectiveness of the approach.

Keywords: Blockchain · Access control · Access logging

1 Introduction

Before sharing data with third parties, organizations participating to a distributed environment would like to agree with them on the processing of this data, so that they can verify if an access intent is legitimate or not. These organizations would also like to know who has processed this data, by keeping immutable traces of every access intent and effective access. This requires access *logging*, i.e., to maintain a complete history of data access for auditing usages. The traditional use of third-party cloud storage services has resulted in isolated (and centralized) data silos, where users (both individuals and enterprises) have limited control over their data and over how it is used: access logs are generated by these services, such that users have to trust the cloud and application providers about the integrity and security of those access logs. In this context, distributed ledger technology (blockchains) has gained significant interest with applications in cryptocurrencies, healthcare [3,5], or IoT [4] to cite a few.

S. Marrone et al. (Eds.): EDCC 2022 Workshops, CCIS 1656, pp. 5–17, 2022.
https://doi.org/10.1007/978-3-031-16245-9_1

We propose AuditTrust, a system for secure and trustworthy data access and access logging in a zero-trust distributed environment. AuditTrust is implemented using a combination of decentralized and secure protocols and technologies, and in particular the Hyperledger Besu blockchain, the IPFS decentralized storage service, the Intel SGX trusted execution environment, and the Vault secret management software. Besides its prototype implementation, AuditTrust is intended also as a reference architecture that can find uses in diverse application domains where data needs to be shared between mutually mistrusting entities.

The remainder of this paper is organized as follows. We present in Sect. 2 a motivating scenario allowing to detail our problem statement through a use case. Section 3 explains why this topic is of interest, and discusses the state of the art related to similar use cases. Section 4 provides details about AuditTrust's architecture and design, Sect. 5 describes our implementation and the evaluation of our system. We conclude this paper in Sect. 6.

2 Use Case: Problem Statement and Motivation

We detail in this section a specific use case, which we use as a motivational example to define our problem statement.

In this use case, several organizations, referring to both public and private sectors (e.g., city authorities, police, a smart traffic company, . . .) would like to access traffic data (e.g., data from CCTV cameras) managed by a traffic monitoring company operating in a specific city. Access to this data is governed by a mutually signed contract between one of these organizations and the company offering the traffic monitoring service. Once shared, this data can be processed by those who have access to it at their destination system. Without proper control of data access and usage at these destination systems, data can be easily shared with a third-party system. This can lead to a data breach and to serious legal consequences. To prevent that, access and usage of data should be auditable in a secure and trustworthy way by any organization participating to the system. To this end, there is a need to have an *audit tool* able to trace any access to the shared data in a trusted and transparent manner, by providing *immutable* access logs. Such an audit tool does not only allow verifying whether there has been suspicious activity inside the system but also to audit the access to shared data within a given time interval. As the organizations are both independent and mutually mistrusting, this audit tool (relying on access logs) cannot be managed by one single entity and the application itself implementing this tool cannot be trusted; rather, the management of such a tool should be decentralized. This decentralization is also necessary to be able to scale up the tool to higher volumes and larger systems, and to make it resilient through redundancy.

Our goal for AuditTrust is to build trust in data shared between mutually mistrusting entities (or participants) in a distributed environment. Typical data being shared could be videos or images originating from smart cities and used notably by smart traffic applications. However, the proposed solution can be used in any application domains, beyond a smart traffic use case. We consider two kinds of mutually mistrusting actors: 1 data consumers (**DCs**) are entities processing data, and 2 data owners (**DOs**), who obtain data, e.g., from traffic monitoring, and share it with DCs. Naturally, a DO might not want to provide the same access to every DC and for every piece of data: each shared piece of data is subject to a role-based access control (RBAC) policy according to which access rights are granted. This policy holds for a bounded amount of time and defines the role or category of users (representing the DC's business function) who are authorized to access the data.

In this use case, building trust in data means that 1 only authorized users are able to access the data according to the policy defined by the data owner. This policy must hold only for a certain duration and for a given role (representing a data consumer's business function), and 2 the access logs on which the audit tool relies cannot be tampered (corrupted). An adversary might try to impersonate another (legitimate) user or compromise any computer system on which the audit tool is available. We also assume that neither the client application (to which a user connects to for interacting with the system) nor the host machines (and operating systems) are trusted.

3 Related Work

Data auditing solutions were previously described in the literature [1,2], although none matches exactly the requirements resulting from our use case.

PrivacyGuard by Xiao et al. [1] implements mechanisms for preserving data integrity and data confidentiality without referring to a trusted third party in the context of data sharing in a cloud environment. PrivacyGuard uses two domains, a control plane and a data plane. The former is related to blockchain interactions and especially to the deployment and execution of smart contracts; the latter is related to the use of a trusted execution environment (TEE) on the cloud for decryption purposes and data processing. PrivacyGuard takes into account more attacks than what we require (e.g., delayed computation in a trusted execution environment or TEE), but is also costlier to operate due to the intensive usage of the blockchain and smart contracts. Each access intent will lead to a smart contract transaction whereas in our solution, a smart contract transaction (publication of an access log) relates to a large batch of access intents. However, PrivacyGuard is easier to deploy because it does not require a specific audit tool: the distributed ledger is the access log itself.

Liang et al. [2] propose ProvChain, a decentralized solution based on own-Cloud to collect and verify the history of all modifications made on shared data. However, their approach assumes some trust relationships, as it relies on an auditor designated by the data provider for verifying data modifications. The scope of the implementation of their solution is also restricted to ownCloud as it requires ownCloud's hooks mechanism. Furthermore, only the provenance data is really decentralized: in ProvChain, Liang et al. [2] rely on a trusted entity to audit data. In our solution, the audit tool can be executed by any participant and does not need to rely on a trusted entity.

Miyachi and Mackey [5] propose 3 different models of decentralized data sharing solutions for healthcare applications, depending on the nature of the data, their purposes, and the applicable regulations. Among these models, the one related to consumer health information (CHI) is similar to our use case: it is used for sharing data, based on a decentralized storage system and TEEs. However, the authors do not consider the same trust model, which impacts the type of blockchain solution they can use. The CHI model allows, indeed, the use of a consortium blockchain where the governance is assigned to a specific group of organizations, an assumption we do not make for AuditTrust.

Wang *et al.* [6] also propose a solution for sharing data in a decentralized manner, with access control mechanisms as well as encryption for preserving data confidentiality. Similarly to the approach of Miyachi and Mackey [5], this solution does not implement an auditing mechanism.

AuditTrust relies on off-chain computation using a TEE. We are not the first to propose to combine the advantages of blockchain processing and the use of a TEE. Ekiden [8] offloads computation from blockchain nodes to a collection of computing nodes, so that the blockchain is solely used as persistent state storage. IRON [9] and Ryoan [10] also combine blockchain and TEE to allow computation on encrypted data through *functional encryption*, following access control that leverage a blockchain. Lastly, Intel introduced in 2018 a solution called Private Data Objects (PDOs) [11], based on TEE and a distributed ledger (Hyperleder Sawtooth). PDOs execute smart contract functions off-chain (within an Intel SGX enclave), while the outputs are stored on the blockchain.

4   AuditTrust: Design and Reference Architecture

In this section, we present the technical solutions for the realization of Audit-Trust and our reference architecture of the tool with all its security components. We will present an implementation of this architecture in Sect. 5. Audit-Trust consists of two key constituents: (1) secure data sharing (i.e. unauthorized access to shared data not possible) and (2) trustworthy access and usage auditing (i.e. access log manipulation not possible). We detail these in the following.

Secure Data Sharing. The enforcement of access/usage policies is necessary before data reaches its destination (i.e., at the DC, data consumer). To this end, we propose to use a role-based access control model expressed in a smart contract to control access to shared data. Roles and policies are defined and represented by smart contracts, allowing all parties to have the same information. Each time a data consumer requests access to some data, this access intent is recorded in the current access log (generated at the data consumer node before being shared with other participants). Each access intent is protected with RSA encryption, relying on the public key of the data owner. To gain access to the file, the local access log first needs to be uploaded to the off-chain platform. From this, a hash can be computed and then can be published on the blockchain, for sharing this access log file with other participants.

When the hash of the access log has been published on the blockchain, the data owner will retrieve the encrypted access log on the off-chain platform. Then, the DO will decrypt and verify the access intents related to its files. This verification process consists of two steps: 1 identity verification and 2 access verification. If the access intent is valid, the data owner will authorize the data consumer to access one of its files.

The data is stored on the off-chain platform and it is protected with a symmetric key issued by the data owner. Instead of transferring the entire file, which would make us lose the benefits of using an off-chain platform, the data owner only sends the cryptography key. However, to preserve the confidentiality of the key, this exchange occurs between secure enclaves hosted in trusted execution environments (TEE). This ensures that the key itself is not accessible to the user (data consumer) itself or to its surrounding software stack, and that the key is used to produce a cleartext version of the file for local use only. Once the enclave on the consumer side has received the key, the file is decrypted inside the enclave and exposed to the user space.

Access and Usage Auditing. To realize trustworthy access and usage auditing, we rely on raw access log stored on the distributed off-chain platform. The address (content identifier) usable to retrieve the log as well as a hash of its content must be stored in an immutable database, which is why we leverage a blockchain for this purpose. The auditing process is simple. First, we retrieve the raw access log and produce a hash-value of it based on a selected cryptographic hashing function. Then, we retrieve the corresponding hash-value stored on blockchain. If they match (hash-value of raw access log on local device and its corresponding hash-value stored in blockchain), there is no tampering, else, tampering occurred. AuditTrust supports two types of audits:

- Total audit: this audit will check the integrity of all access logs available on the off-chain platform and their associated hash published on the blockchain. It outputs a binary value (tampered or not tampered).
- Partial audit: this audit is focused on the data usage control of a specific file. Given two timestamps, it will find all the access logs published during this interval and related to the particular file.

4.1   Reference Architecture

In this section, we present a short description of AuditTrust's high-level architecture. Figure 1 complements this section with a graphical representation of the architecture components. Note that we defer the discussion of the implementation (technologies) for these components to Sect. 5.

The AuditTrust architecture is formed of the following key components:

1. A **front-end** application used by users (both data owner and data consumer). This interface allows the user to connect to different modules of the system, including the database, the service backend, but also the auditing tools. Via

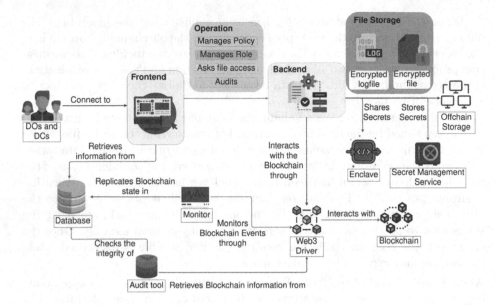

Fig. 1. Global architecture of AuditTrust, representing from a high-level perspective its core components.

this frontend, a user can also manage data access/usage policy and perform auditing on data access if it is authorized to do so.

2. The **back-end**, with different drivers/interfaces, interacts with the different modules of the system such as the blockchain monitoring tool, the blockchain itself, or the off-chain storage and secret management service for managing security key and other credentials.

3. An **off-chain storage** system is responsible for storing durably and reliably data off-chain, implementing the necessary level of redundancy and distribution of the data. It is used for storing *both* encrypted shared data and encrypted access logs.

4. The **audit tool** module is responsible for data access and usage auditing. It interacts with both the database, storing the state of the blockchain transaction, and with the blockchain system through a blockchain driver.

5. Finally, the **blockchain** is used to store the hash-value of the access logs and enables a transparent auditing process.

4.2   Security Mechanisms

In this section, we present several security mechanisms adopted in the design of AuditTrust. The design and implementation of AuditTrust required carefully thinking of a number of security aspects (establishment of secure communication channels and APIs, secure file transfer protocols, or key management) that employ traditional techniques and best practices but will not be discussed in the present paper due to space limitations. We focus instead on aspects that are specific to AuditTrust.

Access Control Management. Proper access control is a critical security feature to allow secure data sharing. We analyzed various access control models when designing AuditTrust (such as discretionary access control - DAC - or mandatory access control - MAC -), and concluded that role-based access control (RBAC) was the most suitable and matches the requirements of our use case. RBAC [7] is a well-known access control model where access permission is granted based on role of user(s)/people in an organization, for instance, users can have a role of employee, administrator, ... RBAC provides an easy way for the user and access rule management since a user is not connected directly to the access rule: the access rule is associated only with role. This means that, to grant or revoke a user's access rights, we need to simply remove the user from the role they belong. When data is shared with data consumers, the access permission is defined based on the role of users belonging to the data consumer organization. This offers freedom for data consumer to assign, un-assign, and reassign a user to that role without affecting the access control policy defined by data owner. This is particularly beneficial when there is a change in user and role structure in the data consumer organization.

Implementing RBAC with Smart Contracts. In AuditTrust, RBAC is used for expressing access control policies. The RBAC policy is then transformed into a RBAC smart contract, which is considered as an agreement between data owner and data consumer. This idea was taken from Cruz *et al.* [12] and implemented in AuditTrust. This smart contract is only executed when new policies are created, updated or deleted. This provides transparency to all involved parties, while avoiding important costs of calling the contract for every access authorization. Based on information from the contract, any party can verify each access intent and enforce the RBAC.

Secure File/Secret Storage. For preserving the confidentiality of data (files and access logs), we use symmetric and asymmetric (RSA) encryption. We generate a symmetric key per shared file. We also encrypt access logs but, in this case, every entry of these files is only readable by the involved parties (a DO and one or several DCs included in the concerned role) and is encrypted with RSA using the DO's public key. The use of encryption enables a DO to share files with a DC, and a DC to audit logs, but bears a risk that the key present in memory of one of the involved DC party will leak and be used to access data without authorization and without logging by malevolent parties. To prevent this risk, AuditTrust relies on a trusted execution environment or TEE. A TEE can execute code (a so-called secure *enclave*) that is certified and can be provisioned with secrets (here, the symmetric key) without revealing these secrets to the machine hosting the enclave or its operating system. The sharing of symmetric keys happens between secure enclaves in TEEs on both sides and the cleartext data is exported, without the key, to regular memory.

Blockchain Usage. AuditTrust leverages a blockchain for two primary purposes. First, it is used as a immutable storage medium to store roles and policies as well as indexing information (content identifiers and hash values) allowing to retrieve content for DC and DO alike. The immutability of the blockchain storage is a necessary asset for a trustworthy auditing process. Second, the blockchain is used as a shared execution medium supporting smart contracts for the management of access control, i.e., setting rules, roles, and associated policies. The execution of these operations is auditable by any party ensuring the transparency of the information exchange agreement between DO and DC.

5   Prototype Implementation and Evaluation

We discuss in this section the implementation of the reference architecture presented for AuditTrust in the previous section, and motivate the technological choices for its different modules.

Blockchain Selection. A large number of blockchain technologies exist, targeting different membership models (open vs. consortium) and deployment models (public vs. private). An important selection criteria for AuditTrust was that the blockchain used should support *immediate finality*, i.e., the fact that a block appended to the chain (and the transactions therein) are never revoked and cancelled later, as can happen with fork events in most open, public blockchains such as "classical" Ethereum. Other important criteria was the compatibility with common toolsets and languages used for smart contracts, and the ability to support various deployment models in the future (i.e., not to be "vendor-locked" in a private solution).

We selected Hyperledger Besu, an Ethereum client supporting both public and private deployments. We use Besu with IBFT 2.0 [13], a proof-of-authority Byzantine fault-tolerant (BFT) algorithm, ensuring immediate finality.

We developed different contracts to handle policy management by data owners (DO), and by specific users of a data consumer (DC) organization:

- DataOwner: There is one smart contract of this type deployed per DO. This smart contract handles all policies issued by a data owner and all actions related to the management of policies;
- DataConsumer: One smart contract of this type is deployed every time a role is created by a DC;
- DataConsumerOrganisation: This smart contract is used for periodically sending access logs to the blockchain, by tracking and aggregating access logs for all managed roles instead of publishing them independently, which would increase the transaction fees of the solution. This smart contract is also responsible for validating the organization's roles.

Off-Chain Storage and Anchorage on the Blockchain. Storing data directly on the blockchain is undesirable and would not scale to the requirements of AuditTrust. It is also undesirable to store data in a centralized location or even at a pre-defined consortium organization under our zero-trust assumption. We use instead a decentralized storage system that does not rely on pairwise trust relations between entities of the system. We selected IPFS [14] for this purpose, one of the currently most popular decentralized store. We point out that any store offering a minimalistic put/get interface could be used in replacement. IPFS addresses data in a content-centric fashion, i.e., the content identifier of a file its the hash of its content. IPFS handles the replication and diffusion of data such that deletion or eclipsing by an adversary requires significant computational and communication power.

For each uploaded file, the content identifier (hash of the file) is published on-chain. This "anchorage" of off-chain data to in-chain records allows checking for data integrity and ensuring availability [15]. As IPFS is distributed and decentralized, data availability is also preserved, which is especially important for files such as access logs. A final positive aspect of decentralized off-chain storage is to avoid having a single point of failure.

Trusted Execution Environment (TEE). The two major choices for TEEs at our disposal from a material perspective or allowing a simulation are ARM TrustZone and Intel SGX. For the purpose of AuditTrust, the features offered are equivalent (even if the programming model differs). We considered both options in the implementation of AuditTrust and settled on Intel SGX due to the simpler programming environment and existence of more complete support libraries. We used specifically the Ego Go library for the Go language [16]. We point out that a production implementation of AuditTrust would probably have to realize a thorough analysis of the library safety as previous work found several weaknesses in other, similar solutions [17].

Client Application. Depending on the type of the user, several operations are possible through the client application. If the user is a data consumer, she can create and manage roles, demand access to some shared file, or access a shared file once access has been validated by AuditTrust. If the user is a data owner, he can create and manage policies for enforcing the RBAC mechanism as explained earlier. Both data consumer and data owner can audit the solution to check if any tampering occurred (resolution or penalization of such occurrences are out of scope of the present paper but would typically leverage on-chain proof-of-misbehavior checking using another smart contract).

Whenever a data consumer wants to access a particular file, an entry is appended in the current access log. This access log is published on the blockchain at periodic intervals. Once the access log is published, the data owner system performs verifications to see if these accesses were legitimate or not. These verifications are composed of two steps: (1) the verification of the identity of the data consumer through a signature mechanism and (2) the verification of the access, i.e. making sure that a policy authorizing this access exists and is still valid. This mechanism incentivizes DC organizations to publish the hash of this access log file on the blockchain because until then its users are unable to access any file.

Once the access is validated by the DO, the DC who made the request can contact the DO node to retrieve the key associated with the file. The DO node will again perform the identity verification, as mentioned before, to make sure it does not share any information with a malicious or unauthorized entity. If the verification phase is successful, both the DO and the DC will attest enclaves in a pair-wise fashion (for SGX, this step requires using an Intel-provided service to attest the genuineness of the communicating SGX enclave and of its running code). Once enclaves are validated, both parties exchange necessary keys over a secure channel visible to only the enclave code.

5.1   Evaluation

Testing Environment. We use a setup environment with 4 virtualized machines on a single host. This host is equipped with a AMD 5800 h 8-core, 16-thread CPU, 32 GB of RAM, and fast NVMe SSD for storage. In addition to the four VMs hosted by KVM, the host runs simple Python scripts to orchestrate the evaluation. Each VM is allocated 2 virtual cores, 5 GB of RAM and 20 GB of disk space. Each virtual host is similar with a Hyperledger Besu node, an IPFS node, and other services implemented as web services. As the CPU does not support SGX, we employ the SGX emulation functionality of the Ego Go library [16].

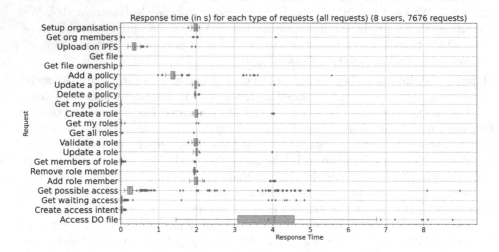

Fig. 2. Global overview of the response time (the vertical bar represents the median and the green triangle is the mean). (Color figure online)

Results. Figure 2 presents the distribution of response times for the various operations involved in the AuditTrust workflows. The latency of the different operations is impacted by calls to the blockchain (and the subsequent wait for the corresponding transaction to appear as finalized in a block), and calls to IPFS to lookup data. Operations are all successful with a majority under 3 s of latency and an average of 3.89 s. The `sign` method, which creates an access intent, is the fastest with an average of 0.03 s.

The majority of requests that interact with the blockchain with a single transaction (e.g., update a policy, role validation, and other management requests.) take a similar time (around two seconds, which is the period of generation of blocks by Besu). The role creation call that requires a slightly more complex call on a smart contract and shows slightly higher variability. Other requests that only require reading the content of the chain replicated in the local database (e.g., getting the file ownership, get the list of roles or retrieving the last state of the solution.), have negligible latency, with the exception of getting the possible access that needs to verify if an existing access intent or authorized access does not exist already; in contrast to queries that only replicate the state of the blockchain without additional verifications. Furthermore, this request, but not only, suffers from the limited performance of the hardware used in our test environment. We also observe that the main function, accessing a file of a data owner by a data consumer, may take a relatively significant time. This is explained by two factors. First, the establishment of secure enclaves on both sides (emulated by Ego Go [16]) and the actual exchange of secrets take time, about 1 to 2 s in total. Second, the relative load on the machine increases due to the in-enclave decryption of the file, leading to throttling mechanisms to trigger to avoid overloading the system in other modules. Overall, our evaluation shows that the cost of auditing and access mediated by a blockchain is not insignificant but remains justified for the level of security that it brings.

Discussion. Our evaluation already provides interesting preliminary results but more extensive tests with a distributed testbed would be necessary to evaluate AuditTrust in a production-like environment. We expect, nonetheless, that the availability of more resources per service (instead of sharing resources for different services in the same VM, and between VMs in the same host) will only provide enhanced performance, e.g., by allowing to decrease the default inter-block period in Besu.

We also note that performance is impacted by some convenience implementation choices and in particular the use of a synchronous communication pattern between our modules, e.g., between the back-end and the IPFS Web3 access library, or between the front-end and back-end components. We believe, nonetheless, that the refactoring of AuditTrust to support asynchronous calls does not incur more than engineering and implementation challenges, and that our proof-of-concept implementation validates the approach.

6 Conclusion

Sharing data and controlling its usage in a distributed context, when participants are mutually mistrustful, is a real challenge. Defining how this data can be processed through strict access control rules, and being able to audit its usage transparently with confidentiality and integrity in a distributed environment where participants do not trust each other is not a trivial problem.

This paper addresses this challenge by designing and prototyping a solution based on recent decentralized and zero-trust technologies including blockchain, distributed storage, and trusted execution environment in addition to classical cryptography. AuditTrust allows data owners (DOs) and data consumers (DCs) to share and to request access to data, alongside the ability to check for fraudulent accesses within the system. AuditTrust, as shown in the evaluation, works well in a modest distributed setup and even with restrained resources and numerous services running in parallel. The proof-of-concept is also limited in its implementation, a point that we intend to address in our future work as well as with the deployment of a larger proof-of-concept in a smart city scenario.

References

1. Xiao, Y., Zhang, N., Li, J., Lou, W., Hou, Y.T.: PrivacyGuard: enforcing private data usage control with blockchain and attested off-chain contract execution. In: Chen, L., Li, N., Liang, K., Schneider, S. (eds.) ESORICS 2020. LNCS, vol. 12309, pp. 610–629. Springer, Cham (2020). https://doi.org/10.1007/978-3-030-59013-0_30
2. Liang, X., Shetty, S., Tosh, D., Kamhoua, C., Kwiat, K., Njilla, L.: ProvChain: a blockchain-based data provenance architecture in cloud environment with enhanced privacy and availability. In: 17th IEEE/ACM International Symposium on Cluster, Cloud and Grid Computing (CCGRID), pp. 468–477. IEEE (2017)
3. Kuo, T.-T., Kim, H.-E., Ohno-Machado, L.: Blockchain distributed ledger technologies for biomedical and health care applications. J. Am. Med. Inform. Assoc. **24**(6), 1211–1220 (2017)
4. Shafagh, H., Burkhalter, L., Hithnawi, A., Duquennoy, S.: Towards blockchain-based auditable storage and sharing of IoT data. In: Proceedings of the 2017 on Cloud Computing Security Workshop, pp. 45–50 (2017)
5. Miyachi, K., Mackey, T.K.: hOCBS: a privacy-preserving blockchain framework for healthcare data leveraging an on-chain and off-chain system design. Inf. Process. Manag. **58**(3), 102535 (2021)
6. Wang, S., Zhang, Y., Zhang, Y.: A blockchain-based framework for data sharing with fine-grained access control in decentralized storage systems. IEEE Access **6**, 38437–38450 (2018)
7. Sandhu, R.S., Coyne, E.J., Feinstein, H.L., Youman, C.E.: Role-based access control models. Computer **29**(2), 38–47 (1996)
8. Cheng, R., et al.: Ekiden: a platform for confidentiality-preserving, trustworthy, and performant smart contracts. In: 2019 IEEE European Symposium on Security and Privacy (EuroS&P), pp. 185–200 (2019)
9. Fisch, B., Vinayagamurthy, D., Boneh, D., Gorbunov, S.: IRON: functional encryption using Intel SGX. In: ACM SIGSAC Conference on Computer and Communications Security (CCS), pp. 765–782. ACM (2017)
10. Hunt, T., Zhu, Z., Xu, Y., Peter, S., Witchel, E.: Ryoan: a distributed sandbox for untrusted computation on secret data. ACM Trans. Comput. Syst. **35**(4), 13:1–13:32 (2018)
11. Bowman, M., Miele, A., Steiner, M., Vavala, B.: Private data objects: an overview. arXiv, 5 November 2018
12. Cruz, J.P., Kaji, Y., Yanai, N.: RBAC-SC: role-based access control using smart contract. IEEE Access **6**, 12240–12251 (2018). https://doi.org/10.1109/ACCESS.2018.2812844

13. IBFT 2.0 - hyperledger besu. https://besu.hyperledger.org/en/stable/HowTo/Configure/Consensus-Protocols/IBFT/
14. Benet, J.: IPFS-content addressed, versioned, P2P file system. arXiv preprint arXiv:1407.3561 (2014)
15. Eberhardt, J., Heiss, J.: Off-chaining models and approaches to off-chain computations. In: 2nd Workshop on Scalable and Resilient Infrastructures for Distributed Ledgers (SERIAL), pp. 7–12 (2018)
16. EdgeLess systems, Ego-Go library. https://github.com/edgelesssys/ego
17. Liu, W., et al.: Understanding TEE containers, easy to use? Hard to trust. arXiv preprint arXiv:2109.01923 (2021)

Formal Analysis Approach for Multi-layered System Safety and Security Co-engineering

Megha Quamara[1,2]([⊠])(iD), Gabriel Pedroza[1]([⊠])(iD), and Brahim Hamid[2]([⊠])(iD)

[1] Université Paris-Saclay, CEA, List, 91120 Palaiseau, France
{megha.quamara,gabriel.pedroza}@cea.fr
[2] IRIT - University of Toulouse, 118 Route de Narbonne,
31062 Toulouse Cedex 9, France
brahim.hamid@irit.fr

Abstract. Critical domains (like Cyber-Physical Systems-CPSs) have witnessed increased demand for considering both safety and security concerns during the early phases of the System Engineering (SE) process. Particularly, in the design phase, safety and security requirements should cascade down across different system views till the architectural design. However, such an enrichment process is often complex and lacks guidance to precisely specify the corresponding properties and consistently break down high-level system specifications into intricate architecture for a rigorous analysis. To this end, we propose a formal approach pursuing joint analysis of safety and security objectives, specialize-able across different system views. In particular, the approach strives for a multi-layered system representation, integrating mission, functional and component views, and libraries of pre-defined safety and security properties, instantiate-able at each layer. We rely upon the meta-modeling and formal techniques for the specification, conceptual modeling, formal interpretation, and verification of the system w.r.t. the allocated properties. The overall approach is validated using Rodin as an instance of a formal-based tool for properties' verification.

Keywords: Safety · Security · Co-engineering · Design · Analysis · Model-driven engineering · Formal methods

1 Introduction

Modern engineered systems, like Cyber-Physical Systems (CPSs), are becoming increasingly complex due to the integration of a variety of technology, highly networked and with heterogeneous usages and contexts. Despite their enormous potential, deploying such systems in critical applications entails the integration of safety and security concerns in light of their mutual influence. Nevertheless, a joint analysis towards harmonizing safety and security expertise is technically challenging. Particularly, in the design phase, the requirements are broken

S. Marrone et al. (Eds.): EDCC 2022 Workshops, CCIS 1656, pp. 18–31, 2022.
https://doi.org/10.1007/978-3-031-16245-9_2

down from the high-level teleological representations to the detailed technical architecture of the System Under Design (SUD). However, this enrichment process is often complex and lacks guidance for consistent semantic transfer and integration of safety and security concerns/requirements. Besides, conducting design-level properties'[1] verification to increase design trustworthiness, can be error-prone due to ambiguous properties' specifications or biases introduced by non-savvy engineer's interpretation. Moreover, existing System Engineering (SE) approaches exhibit standalone safety and security analyses in many cases [5,7]. As evident in several safety-critical domains (e.g., automotive), an entanglement exists between safety constraints (e.g., messages' latency) and security exigencies (e.g., encryption mechanisms' overhead), and their mutual assurance needs to be verified [15]. In addition, we observe a lack of automated tool support for integrated analysis of the system, safety, and security properties; the disciplines of software architecture, security, and safety engineering are still to be better interfaced regarding their methods and frameworks.

To address the problematics above, we propose a joint design and analysis approach for three-layered system safety and security co-engineering. The work in this paper mainly focuses on (1) the vertical integration of notions for safety and security interplay across different modeling views of the system and (2) emphasizing the formal aspects for properties' representation, verification, and conflict identification. The approach relies on conceptual modeling using existing modeling languages (e.g., Unified Modeling Language (UML) [9]) to describe high-level safety and security objectives, i.e., the positive features or properties, specialize-able across different system views in the context of a three-layered system representation: mission, functional, and component. Besides the typical system's structural and behavioral concerns' analysis [3], we propose to impose a defined set of safety and security objectives' signatures at each layer to check for design conformity and avoid potential conflicts. As a prerequisite, we define interpretation rules for mapping the modeling concepts to their formal-based counterparts relying upon mathematical logic, namely First-Order Logic (FOL) and Modal Logic [4]. Moreover, we use Event-B [1], to obtain a more concrete specification of the system and property conceptual model and the accompanying formal-based tool, namely Rodin [16], to mechanize properties verification and spot inconsistencies at early modeling phases. The approach is illustrated via a Connected Driving Vehicles (CDVs) use case.

The rest of the paper is organized as follows. Section 2 describes the conceptual modeling of the system and safety and security properties. Section 3 presents the formalization of the model using FOL and Modal Logic. Section 4 describes the interpretation of the formalized model into Event-B for supporting properties analysis. Section 5 reviews related works. Finally, Sect. 6 concludes this paper, with perspective work directions.

---

[1] Fundamental well-defined notions that are building blocks upon which high-level requirements can be decomposed and characterized.

2   Multi-layered System Conceptual Model

A conceptual model of a multi-layered system should capture the main concepts and relationships for describing the system in the context of different standards and domain-specific practices. We use UML Class diagrams to describe the conceptual model. Thus, concepts are represented by Classes, concept attributes by Class attributes, and relationships among concepts by links (e.g., association). The Package notation is used to make groupings of the concepts. An excerpt of the graphical representation of the concepts and relationships is given in Fig. 1. In the rest of this section, we outline the different packages. Special attention is given to the concepts that show the essential features of this work. To facilitate readability and comprehension, the attributes of the different concepts and some of the links among the concepts are also described.

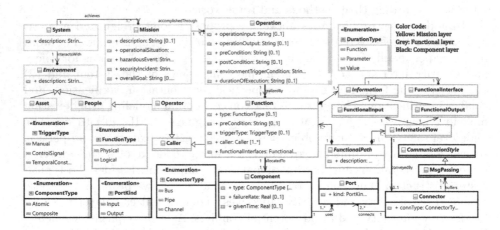

Fig. 1. Excerpt of the multi-layered system specification meta-model.

The proposed conceptual model is divided into four packages: (1) **Mission**, for concepts related to mission engineering; (2) **Functional**, for concepts related to functional engineering; (3) **Component**, for describing component-based engineering; and (4) **Property**, for safety and security aspects capturing and analysis. The *Mission* package contains concepts for offering system's teleological view, such as the *System* (e.g., CDV), *Mission* (system's high-level strategic concerns, e.g., collision avoidance [SAFE_M], ensure authorized actions [SEC_M]), *Operation* (for mission accomplishment, e.g., braking, access provisioning), *Environment* (comprising *People* or *Assets*), etc. The *Functional* package contains all the concepts correlated with the system's functionality, such as the *Function* (system's elementary tasks or services, e.g., perception- or actuation-related), *FunctionalPath* (sequence of functions to realize the operation via *Information-Flows*), etc. The *Component* package contains all the concepts for the system's detailed technical representation, such as the *Component* (self-contained computational elements/physical entities, e.g., sensor), *Ports* (for data exchange), *Connectors* (channels for establishing communication), etc.

Finally, the *Property* package (see Fig. 2) contains all the concepts for safety and security properties capturing and analysis, such as the *PropertyCategoryLibrary* (reusable model libraries for defining high-level properties of the system, function, component, etc.) and *PropertyCategory* (classification of safety and security objectives in a given context). The libraries are subsequently used as external models for capturing the objectives as signatures. We extend some properties (e.g., *Precedence* [8] and *Equivalence* [2]) from the literature by adapting them to the context of our approach. We call these properties the basic ones since they play an elementary role in defining specific safety and security objectives (e.g., *Functional Integrity*) associated with the target SUD.

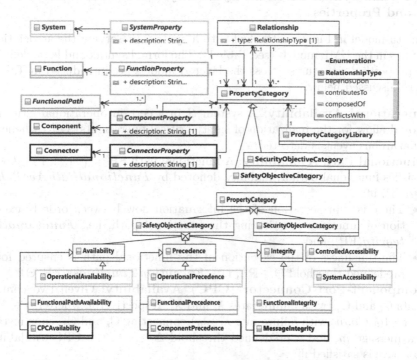

Fig. 2. Safety and security properties' specification meta-model.

Likewise, potential inter- or intra-relationships between safety and security objectives may arise within or across the layers. Thus, we aim to establish an alignment via links between objectives to support further analysis, including safety and security interplay. We define the association (e.g., *dependsUpon*, *conflictsWith*) between these objectives. For example, operational availability (mission layer) *depends upon* functional path availability (functional layer), system accessibility (mission layer) *conflicts with* operational availability (mission layer), etc.

3   Logical Specification

This section presents the formalization of the multi-layered system conceptual model defined in the previous section for rigorous specification and analysis of safety and security objectives. We use FOL and Modal Logic [4] as technology-independent formalisms to incorporate formal syntaxes for the system model and properties belonging to the defined categories. They play as a pivot language that aims to facilitate model interpretation and improve flexibility, *e.g.*, to delegate the properties' analysis to other tooled-formal languages and frameworks. In our context, the analysis has been mechanized, thanks to the Rodin framework, as presented in the next section.

3.1   Formal Syntax for Multi-layered System Specification and Properties

The meta-model in Fig. 1 is attached with a syntax, preserving the associations and types in the UML models (see Table 1). The formal syntax and logic defining some properties' signatures across the layered models are introduced in Table 2 and are discussed below:

- **Operational Availability:** A system S in a certain operational situation should allow for the realization of safety-critical operation(s) Op_j, whenever a hazardous event is detected.
- **Functional Path Availability:** A functional path $FP := (F_1,..., F_k)$, $k \in \mathbb{N}$ satisfies functional path availability denoted by *FunctionalPathAvailability*(FP) iff:
  - There is a preservation of the information flow between orderly execution of functions constituting the functional path, i.e., *FunctionalIntegrity*(FP), and
  - The timeliness of the execution of the functional path is ensured for a predefined threshold $\Theta \in \mathbb{R}^+$, i.e., *ExecutionTimeliness*(FP, Θ).
- **Component-Port-Connector (CPC) Availability:** Given two components C_i and C_j (with failure rates λ_i and λ_j, respectively), where $i, j \in \mathbb{N}$, a connector *Conn* (with failure rate λ_{Conn}) connecting C_i and C_j, time instant t, a message m, and a predefined threshold $\Delta \in \mathbb{R}^+$, the CPC availability objective is satisfied iff:
  - Availability of components is ensured, i.e., *ComponentAvailability*(C_i, λ_i, t),
  - Availability of connector is ensured, i.e., *ConnectorAvailability*(Conn, λ_{Conn}, t),
  - Delivery of critical messages between the components is ensured, i.e., *EventualMessageDelivery*(C_i, C_j, m) (or *BoundedMessageDelivery*(C_i, C_j, m, Δ)), and
  - There exists logical conformity of the component architecture (i.e., configuration) with functional architecture.

– **System Accessibility:** A system S must allow and limit the access of security-critical operation(s) Op_j to only authorized entities (e.g., Operator).

Here, we integrate the formal syntaxes presented in Tables 1 and 2 to define formal semantics for the layered elements. The FOL-based formalism of safety and security objectives' specifications are extended using a range of modalities, including $\circ$ (*next*), $\Diamond$ (*eventually*), $\Diamond_{\leq\Theta}$ (*bounded eventually*, where Θ denotes the threshold or bounded gap between two events/occurrences/actions etc.), and $\Box$ (*always*) for capturing the notion of future [4]. Likewise, $\bullet$, $\blacklozenge$, $\blacklozenge_{\leq\Theta}$, and $\blacksquare$, respectively denote their past counterparts. These are defined on top of standard FOL operators, including $\wedge$ (*conjunction*), $\vee$ (*disjunction*), $\neg$ (*negation*), $\rightarrow$ (*implication*), and $\leftrightarrow$ (*equivalence*). For example, predicates of the form $P \Rightarrow Q$ can be interpreted as $\Box(P \rightarrow \Diamond Q)$. Similarly, predicates of the form $P \Leftrightarrow Q$ can be interpreted as $\Box(P \leftrightarrow Q)$. Here, $\Rightarrow$ means *strongly implies* and $\Leftrightarrow$ means *strongly equivalent*.

Table 1. Excerpt of mapping: three-layered conceptual model $\mapsto$ formal syntax.

Conceptual element	Formal syntax
System	$S := (\{M_i\}, \text{Environment})$, $i \in \{1 \dots \mathbb{N}\}$, Environment $\in \{\text{People, Asset}\}$
Mission	$M_i := (\{Op_j\}, operationalSituation, hazardousEvent, securityIncident, overallGoal)$, $i, j \in \{1 \dots \mathbb{N}\}$
Operation	$Op_j := (operationInput, operationOutput, preCondition, postCondition, environmentTriggerCondition, durationOfExecution, durationType)$, $j \in \{1 \dots \mathbb{N}\}$, $durationType \in \{Function, Parameter, Value\}$
Function	$F_k := (type, preCondition, triggerType, caller, functionalInterfaces, \text{Information})$, $type \in \{Physical, Logical\}$, $triggerType \in \{Manual, ControlSignal, TemporalConstraint\}$, TemporalConstraint $\in \{Duration, TriggerTime\}$, $caller \in \{Operator, F_l, TemporalConstraint\}$, $k, l \in \{1 \dots \mathbb{N}\}$
Information	Information $\in \{\text{FunctionalInput (or } I_k), \text{FunctionalOutput (or } O_k)\}$, $k \in \{1 \dots \mathbb{N}\}$
InformationFlow	InformationFlow $:= (\{(O_i, I_j) \triangleq (F_i, F_j)\} \mid$ FunctionalOutput$[F_i] = O_i$, FunctionalInput$[F_j] = I_j)$, $i, j \in \{1 \dots \mathbb{N}\}$
FunctionalPath	$FP := (F_1, \dots, F_k) \mid \forall(F_k, F_{k+1}), \exists (O_k, I_{k+1}) \in \{(O_i, I_j)\}$, $i, j, k \in \{1 \dots \mathbb{N}\}$
Component	$C_m := (\{P_n\}, type, failureRate, givenTime)$, $m, n \in \{1 \dots \mathbb{N}\}$, $type \in \{Atomic, Composite\}$
Port	$P_n := (kind)$, $n \in \{1 \dots \mathbb{N}\}$, $kind \in \{Input, Output\}$
Connector	Conn $:= (connType, P_n, P_o, \text{CommunicationStyle})$, $connType \in \{Bus, Pipe, Channel\}$, $n, o \in \{1 \dots \mathbb{N}\}$

Table 2. Excerpt of mapping: properties' metamodel $\mapsto$ formal syntax.

Conceptual element	Formal syntax
OperationalAvailability	$(operationalSituation[M_i] \wedge hazardousEvent[M_i]) \Rightarrow$ $accomplishedThrough[M_i, Op_j]$
FunctionalPathAvailability	a) $\boldsymbol{FunctionalIntegrity}$(FP): $\boldsymbol{FunctionalPrecedence}(F_k, F_{k+1})$, $\forall k \in \{1...N-1\}$: $F_j \Rightarrow F_i$ $\boldsymbol{InformationEquivalence}(O_k, I_{k+1})$, $\forall k \in \{1...N-1\}$: $I_j \Leftrightarrow O_i$ b) $\boldsymbol{ExecutionTimeliness}$(FP, Θ): $\mathcal{O}(F_1, F_1, t_1, I_1)$ $\Rightarrow_\Theta \mathcal{O}(F_{k-1}, F_k, t_{2k}, O_k)$
CPCAvailability	a) $\boldsymbol{ComponentAvailability}(C_i, \lambda_i, t)$ b) $\boldsymbol{ConnectorAvailability}(Conn, \lambda_{Conn}, t)$ c) $\boldsymbol{EventualMessageDelivery}(C_i, C_j, m)$: $send(C_i, m) \Rightarrow receive(C_j, m)$ (or $\boldsymbol{BoundedMessageDelivery}(C_i, C_j, m, \Delta)$): $send(C_i, m) \Rightarrow_\Delta receive(C_j, m)$ d) Logical conformity of component architecture with functional architecture
SystemAccessibility	$privilege[Operator, S, Op_j] \Rightarrow access[Operator, Op_j]$

3.2 Safety and Security Interplay

Interplay within Mission Layer. Consider a use case scenario where collision avoidance is the high-level mission of the CDV. The manual triggering of brakes to avoid the collision situation may hinder the denial of manual operation access to the operator in cases where safety is prioritized over security.

In such cases, conflicts between safety (namely operational availability) and security (namely system accessibility) objectives can be identified by analyzing the predicates. More concretely, for any states in which all post-conditions are not satisfied simultaneously. For example, consider the following predicate at the mission layer specification, where $Op_1 :=$ braking and $Op_2 :=$ access provisioning, respectively denote the safety and security-critical operations performed by the CDV for the accomplishment of the mission M_1: collision avoidance:

$$accomplishedThrough[M_1, Op_1, Op_2] \Rightarrow (overallGoal[M_1] \Leftrightarrow$$
$$(\neg postCondition[Op_1] \vee \neg postCondition[Op_2]))$$

Using the semantics defined in Sect. 3.1, the above predicate is specified as:

$$\Box(accomplishedThrough[M_1, Op_1, Op_2] \rightarrow \Diamond(overallGoal[M_1] \leftrightarrow$$
$$(\neg postCondition[Op_1] \vee \neg postCondition[Op_2])))$$

Thus, no simultaneous fulfillment of post-conditions belonging to Op_1 and Op_2 after mission accomplishment shall indicate, in particular, a conflict between the safety and security objectives of the SUD.

Interplay Across Mission and Functional Layers. Consider a situation when the trigger condition of an operation becomes true within the duration of another operation's execution. For example, the premature deployment of the vehicle's airbag during braking, which is still in progress without effective crash condition. In such cases, the conflict may occur at the level of high-level mission specification since the two missions' overall goals may have conflicting requirements.

In such cases, conflicts between objectives can be identified during the operations' (i.e., Op_j) realization to accomplish different missions. Hence, for the overall system model at the mission layer, the following predicate is violated:

$$environmentTriggerCondition[Op_j] \Rightarrow preCondition[Op_j]$$

Using the semantics provided in our context, this predicate is specified as:

$$\Box(environmentTriggerCondition[Op_j] \rightarrow \blacklozenge(preCondition[Op_j]))$$

To illustrate the interplay with the functional layer, we consider a functional path comprising a set of functions (i.e., F_k) and the link *realizedBy* between the operations and the functions. Herein, the assurance of functional integrity for the functional path realizing a sequence of operations is assumed. However, the delay introduced by any constituent function during execution may violate functional path freshness, influencing the timely realization of the operations. Hence, the above mission-layer predicate can be analyzed with the details offered by the functional layer using the following predicate:

$$(triggerTime[F_1] > 0 \wedge trigger[F_2]) \Rightarrow (triggerTime[F_1] + duration < triggerTime[F_2])$$

Using the semantics provided in our context, this predicate can be specified as:

$$\Box((triggerTime[F_1] > 0 \wedge trigger[F_2]) \rightarrow (triggerTime[F_1] + duration < triggerTime[F_2]))$$

Interplay within Component Layer. Consider a scenario comprising three system components, viz. $C_1:=$ processing unit, $C_2:=$ multi-function control unit, and $C_3:=$ brake actuator, engaged in transmitting a message $m:=$ braking command, from C_1 to C_3 via C_2, i.e., $C_1 \longrightarrow_m C_2$ and $C_2 \longrightarrow_m C_3$. Herein, we consider eventual message delivery, influencing CPC Availability, and Non-duplication, influencing message freshness, as the safety and security objectives to be respectively satisfied. We assume that all these components are legitimate. However, if C_2 misbehaves and becomes faulty, it may tamper with m to m', leading to the following flow: $C_1 \longrightarrow_m C_2$ and $C_2 \longrightarrow_{m'} C_3$.

Thus, even after tampering, the non-duplication objective is satisfied as none of the recipients (viz. C_2 and C_3) undergo the repeated transmission of the message. However, the eventual message delivery for m is not satisfied as C_3, the intended recipient, does not receive the original message m. Hence, in such scenarios, the safety and security analysis should not be conducted as standalone but integrated for the assurance of corresponding objectives, especially across the full chain of transmission.

Hence, in our context, for the overall system model targeting the component layer details, the aforementioned aspect can be analyzed via the following predicate:

$$send(C_i, m) \Rightarrow receive(C_j, m) \land \neg(receive(C_i, m))$$

$$send(C_i, m) \Rightarrow receive(C_j, m)$$

Using the semantics provided before, the predicate above can be specified as follows:

$$\square(send(C_i, m) \rightarrow \lozenge(receive(C_j, m)) \land \neg(\blacklozenge(receive(C_i, m))))$$
$$\square(send(C_i, m) \rightarrow \lozenge(receive(C_j, m)) \land \neg(\blacklozenge(receive(C_j, m))))$$

The first predicate is not expected to be satisfied; otherwise, the message sent by C_2 to C_3 is not the same as the one sent by C_1 to C_2. The second predicate should be satisfied whenever the uniqueness of the message is expected to occur.

4   Formal Specification and Analysis in Event-B

In this section, we consider interpreting the system and properties' meta-models and logical specification in the previous section into Event-B [1].

Structural Elements. The multi-layered system model is represented in Event-B via a set of *contexts* and *machines* refined within each layer. The *contexts* are used for the formal declaration of conceptual model elements, both structural and properties, along with the utility constants for generic representation of the elements. Herein, the key elements like Mission, Function, Component, and enumerations are defined as Event-B *sets*, while their attributes are represented as *constants*. Likewise, *axioms* capture the relationship between the elements and their attributes. To model the relation between a set $\mathbb{S}$ (e.g., Environment) and its sub-sets s_1, s_2,..., s_n represented as constants (e.g., People, Asset), we use the *partition* operator, i.e., $partition(\mathbb{S}, s_1, s_2,..., s_n)$. An excerpt of this interpretation is depicted in Listing 1.1.

```
CONTEXT C1MissionView, C2FunctionView, C3ComponentView // for each layer
SETS System, Mission, Environment, Operation, Function, Information,
    TriggerType, Component, Port, Connector, CommunicationStyle,
    ConnectorType
CONSTANTS People, Asset, Manual, ControlSignal, TemporalConstraint,
    FunctionalPath, funcInfo, MsgPassing, Bus, Pipe, Channel, uses,
    connects
AXIOMS
partition(Environment, People, Asset) // Mission layer
partition(TriggerType, Manual, ControlSignal, TemporalConstraint) //
    Functional layer
FunctionalPath ∈ Function ⇸ Function
funcInfo ∈ Function ⟷ Information
funcInfo~ ∈ Information ⇸ Function
```

```
partition(CommunicationStyle, MsgPassing) // Component layer
partition(ConnectorType, Bus, Pipe, Channel)
uses ∈ Component → Port
uses~ ∈ Port ↦ Component
connects ∈ Connector → Port
connects~ ∈ Port ↦ Connector
```

Listing 1.1. Interpretation excerpt: Three-layered system model in Event-B.

Furthermore, *machine* specifications formally capture the desired behavioral aspects of the system as model *invariants*. The abstract machine specification provides an initial setup for the Event-B model that can be refined with concrete details. A machine *sees* a context to use its axioms in conjunction as hypotheses in the mathematical proofs. We define *events* in the machines targeting each layer to capture the state transitions associated with the application of operations, function execution, and CPC-based message transmission. Listing 1.2 depicts an excerpt of this interpretation for the mission layer.

```
MACHINE M1MissionView
SEES C4MissionUtility // Context for utility constants, e.g., s1, m1, o1
VARIABLES operationalSituation, hazardousEvent, overallGoal,
    environmentTriggerCondition, achieves, counter, accomplishedThrough,
    interactsWith
EVENTS HazardousEventPresence
WHEN
    operationalSituation = {m1 ↦ TRUE}
    hazardousEvent = {m1 ↦ FALSE}
    overallGoal = {m1 ↦ FALSE}
    environmentTriggerCondition = {o1 ↦ FALSE}
    achieves = {s1 ↦ m1}
    counter > 0 // An integer counter for capturing timeout
THEN
    hazardousEvent :- {m1 ↦ TRUE}
    environmentTriggerCondition :- {o1 ↦ TRUE}
    accomplishedThrough :- {m1 ↦ o1}
    interactsWith :- {s1 ↦ a1}
    counter :- counter - 1
```

Listing 1.2. Excerpt of an Event-B machine at the mission layer specification.

Properties Specification. We define the safety and security objectives presented in Sect. 3.1 in Event-B as model *invariants* to verify that the defined events satisfy them during system model verification at different layers. Herein, the invariants are represented as the combination of state variables (i.e., the concept attributes) and logic symbols, i.e., propositions (e.g., $\Rightarrow$, $\Leftrightarrow$) and predicates (e.g., $\forall$, $\exists$) between them. The *guards* restrict the values of the variables as enabling conditions for the events. An excerpt of the Event-B interpretation for the *Operational Availability* objective is given in Listing 1.3.

```
INVARIANTS
∀m.∃o.m∈ Mission ∧ o ∈ Operation ∧ (operationalSituation[{m}] = {TRUE} ∧
    hazardousEvent[{m}] = {TRUE}) ⇒ accomplishedThrough[{m}] = {o}
```

Listing 1.3. Operational availability objective as Event-B invariant.

Of particular interest here, objectives like *Functional Path Availability* are defined as extensions of basic properties like *Functional Precedence, Information*

Equivalence, and *Execution Timeliness*. Then they are captured in Event-B via invariant decomposition, where each basic property is associated individually with an invariant.

Properties Analysis. To reason and verify the invariants, we rely upon mathematical proofs comprising a set of rules. These rules are based upon the convention of Proof-Obligations (POs) supported by the Rodin platform. A PO is generated for every invariant that can be affected by an event, i.e., the invariant contains variables that an event can change. The hypothesis for these POs relies upon the satisfaction of all the invariants (including behavioral, safety and security objectives, and gluing) and the validity of the guards restricting the values of the variables before the triggering of events in every reachable state of the system. The correctness of the instantiated model is dependent on ninety-one POs[2] that are related to mission accomplishment through the execution of the operation, function, and CPC-centric events.

To illustrate the analysis, we present the extraction of the PO for the satisfaction of the operational availability objective as an invariant, relying upon two invariants INV1 and INV2, and a theorem THM, as follows:

1. **MissionAllocation (INV1):** $\forall m \in$ Mission, $\exists o \in$ Operation $|$ ((operationalSituation[m] $\wedge$ hazardousEvent[m]) $\Leftrightarrow$ (preCondition[o] $\wedge$ environmentTriggerCondition[o])) $\Rightarrow$ accomplishedThrough[m] = o; holds for all the events.
2. **MissionConsistency (INV2):** $\forall m \in$ Mission, (operationalSituation[m] $\wedge \neg$ hazardousEvent[m]) $\Rightarrow \neg$ overallGoal[m]; holds for all the events.
3. **MissionAccomplishment (THM):** $\forall m \in$ Mission, o $\in$ Operation $|$ (accomplishedThrough[m] = o) $\Rightarrow$ (postCondition[o] $\Leftrightarrow$ overallGoal[m]); a derived axiom that relies upon INV1 and INV2.

Likewise, the properties' conflict identification predicate presented in Sect. 3.2, for instance, at the mission layer, is presented in the Listing 1.4 as an Event-B invariant.

```
INVARIANTS
∀m.∃o1.∃o2.m ∈ Mission ∧ o1 ∈ Operation ∧ o2 ∈ Operation ∧
    accomplishedThrough[{m}] = {o1, o2} ⇒ (overallGoal[{m}] = {TRUE} ∧ (¬
    postCondition[{o1}] = {TRUE} ∨¬postCondition[{o2}] = {TRUE}))
```

Listing 1.4. Mission layer properties conflict identification predicate as Event-B invariant.

For the safety and security missions SAFE_M and SEC_M, respectively, in the use case (see Sect. 2), the PO corresponding to the invariant in Listing 1.4 is discharged, depicting a potential conflict between braking and access provisioning operations. The reason can be attributed to the lack of privilege to the operator to realize the braking operation manually (i.e., Operator $\mapsto$ CDV1 $\mapsto$ Braking $\notin$ *privilege*).

---

[2] Distribution of POs: Variable initialization (32), System specification (48), Safety and security invariants (11).

5   Related Work and Positioning

So far, numerous solutions have been proposed in the literature to address safety and security concerns during the SE process (e.g., [17]). However, the challenge is reconciling interdisciplinary knowledge, domain-oriented goals, and standalone practices towards effective co-engineering. This section dwells on some related works and positions our approach, emphasizing system conceptual modeling frameworks, design and analysis methods, and tooled-formal methods.

The mission is defined as a context-oriented and multi-paradigmatic concept in [13] (e.g., goal and object-oriented) that facilitates entanglement of system functionality with architectural design process. In light of this, the authors in [6] presented a mission-based process for wave development cycle, thus resulting in less generic than our approach. Nonetheless, these works cover only the requirement engineering phase. To address high-level functional specification and application of safety-oriented practices during critical systems' design, Design Space Exploration (DSE) capabilities are used in [18]. Component-based design techniques and frameworks are proposed concerning safety [14] and security [5] requirements in automotive CPSs applications by modeling and analyzing real-time component interactions. Our work is aligned with these X-by-design approaches and aims, additionally, to provide generic and specializable means to integrate safety and security aspects irrespective of the design flow (top-down or bottom-up).

Tooled-formal methods, when used in the engineering process of safety- and security-critical systems, increase confidence in the aspects, e.g., properties, defined by the respective standards [11,12]. Several works demonstrate the use of the Event-B formal method for rigorous analysis of safety [10] and security [17] concerns. However, these works are constrained by the granularity level and concepts chosen for modeling what imposes requirements to be specified at the same level. The independent formal interpretation of the layers facilitates engineers to use them in standalone or coupled mode, adequate for granularity and analysis needs. Being technology-agnostic, the proposed approach provides further flexibility regarding the choice of specification/modeling languages and Validation and Verification (V&V) tool support.

6   Conclusion and Perspectives

We have proposed a joint design and analysis formal approach for integrated specification, modeling, and verification of safety and security properties. In this work, we mainly focused on the formalization aspects to address the ambiguities associated with the properties' specification and their interpretation w.r.t. the system design to conduct provable, sound analyses. To this end, the approach leveraged multi-layered system conceptual modeling, targeting high-level mission, functional, and detailed CPC-related concepts and their relationships. Indeed, the incorporated notions include properties' categories and signatures, a basis for joint safety and security analyses. Subsequently, the logical specification of the conceptual model was described using set theories, FOL, and

Modal Logic as technology-independent formalisms. Based on this formalization, a model interpretation into Event-B was defined to conduct automated verification of safety and security objectives' signatures. However, being aware of the possibility of more complex configurations, like use cases calling upon a large set of objectives (e.g., those within the *Freshness* category), we plan to explore and analyze them to increase the approach's confidence. We are also interested in investigating the negative view of the properties where fault/failure/hazard and threat models are introduced.

References

1. Abrial, J.R., et al.: Rodin: an open toolset for modelling and reasoning in Event-B. Int. J. Softw. Tools Technol. Transfer **12**(6), 447–466 (2010)
2. Babel, K., Cheval, V., Kremer, S.: On the semantics of communications when verifying equivalence properties. J. Comput. Secur. **28**(1), 71–127 (2020)
3. Bau, J., Mitchell, J.C.: Security modeling and analysis. IEEE Secur. Priv. **9**(3), 18–25 (2011)
4. Bull, R., Segerberg, K.: Basic modal logic. In: Gabbay, D., Guenthner, F. (eds.) Handbook of Philosophical Logic, pp. 1–88. Springer, Dordrecht (1984). https://doi.org/10.1007/978-94-009-6259-0_1
5. Chattopadhyay, A., Lam, K.Y., Tavva, Y.: Autonomous vehicle: security by design. IEEE Trans. Intell. Transp. Syst. **22**, 7015–7029 (2020)
6. Cherfa, I., Belloir, N., Sadou, S., Fleurquin, R., Bennouar, D.: Systems of systems: from mission definition to architecture description. Syst. Eng. **22**(6), 437–454 (2019)
7. De Miguel, M.A., Briones, J.F., Silva, J.P., Alonso, A.: Integration of safety analysis in model-driven software development. IET Softw. **2**(3), 260–280 (2008)
8. Dwyer, M.B., Avrunin, G.S., Corbett, J.C.: Patterns in property specifications for finite-state verification. In: Proceedings of the 21st International Conference on Software Engineering, pp. 411–420 (1999)
9. Fuentes-Fernández, L., Vallecillo-Moreno, A.: An introduction to UML profiles. UML Model Eng. **2**(6–13), 72 (2004)
10. Hong, Z., Lili, X.: Application of software safety analysis using Event-B. In: 2013 IEEE Seventh International Conference on Software Security and Reliability Companion, pp. 137–144. IEEE (2013)
11. ISO 26262–1:2018 Road vehicles - Functional safety (2018). https://www.iso.org/standard/43464.html
12. ISO/IEC 27000:2018 Information technology - Security techniques - Information security management systems (2018). https://www.iso.org/standard/73906.html
13. Letier, E., Van Lamsweerde, A.: Deriving operational software specifications from system goals. ACM SIGSOFT Softw. Eng. Notes **27**(6), 119–128 (2002)
14. Masrur, A., Kit, M., Matěna, V., Bureš, T., Hardt, W.: Component-based design of cyber-physical applications with safety-critical requirements. Microprocess. Microsyst. **42**, 70–86 (2016)
15. Pedroza, G., Apvrille, L., Knorreck, D.: AVATAR: a SysML environment for the formal verification of safety and security properties. In: 2011 11th Annual International Conference on New Technologies of Distributed Systems, pp. 1–10. IEEE (2011)

16. Rodin: Rodin Platform (2021). https://wiki.event-b.org/
17. Vistbakka, I., Troubitsyna, E.: Towards a formal approach to analysing security of safety-critical systems. In: 2018 14th European Dependable Computing Conference (EDCC), pp. 182–189. IEEE (2018)
18. Wan, J., Canedo, A., Al Faruque, M.A.: Cyber-physical codesign at the functional level for multidomain automotive systems. IEEE Syst. J. **11**(4), 2949–2959 (2015)

Workshop on Dynamic Risk managEment for Autonomous Systems (DREAMS)

First Workshop on Dynamic Risk managEment for AutonoMous Systems (DREAMS)

Workshop Description

Autonomous systems have enormous potential and they are bound to be a major driver in future economical and societal transformations. Their key trait is that they pursue and achieve their more or less explicitly defined goals independently and without human guidance or intervention. In contexts where safety, or other critical properties, need to be guaranteed it is, however, presently hardly possible to exploit autonomous systems to their full potential. Unknowns and uncertainties are induced due to high complexity of the autonomous behaviors, the utilized technology, and the volatile and highly complex system contexts. These characteristics render the base assumptions of established assurance methodologies (and standards) void, hence new approaches need to be investigated. One general approach to deal with such unknowns and uncertainties is to shift parts of the development time assurance activities into runtime.

Giving autonomous systems risk management skills means empowering them to monitor their environments (i.e., other collaborating systems as well as the physical environment), analyze and reason about implications regarding risks, and, execute actions to control risks ensuring that all risks are acceptable at any time – thus conducting dynamic risk management (DRM). DRM has the potential to not only outright enable certain types of systems or applications but also to significantly increase the performance of already existing ones. This is due to the fact that by resolving unknowns and uncertainties at runtime it will be possible to get rid of worst case assumptions that typically detriment the systems performance properties. The DREAMS workshop aims to explore concepts and techniques for realizing DRM. It invites experts, researchers, and practitioners for presentations and in-depth discussions about prediction models for risk identification, integration between strategic, tactical, and operational risk management, architectures for dynamic risk management, and V&V of dynamic risk management.

The DREAMS workshop aims at bringing together communities from diverse disciplines, such as safety engineering, runtime adaptation, predictive modeling, and control theory, and from different application domains, such as automotive, healthcare, manufacturing, agriculture, and critical infrastructures.

Organization

Program Chairs

Rasmus Adler   Fraunhofer IESE, Germany
Richard Hawkins   University of York/Assuring Autonomy
     International Program, UK
Philipp Schleiß   Fraunhofer IKS, Germany

Program Committee

Mohammed Abuteir   TTTech, Austria
Eric Armengaud   Armengaud Innovate GmbH, Austria
Ricque Bertrand   Safran Electronics & Defense, France
Simon Burton   Fraunhofer IKS, Germany
Huascar Espinoza   KDT JU, France
Patrik Feth   Sick AG, Germany
Thomas Freudenmann   EDI GmbH, Germany
Roman Gansch   Bosch, Germany
Phil Kopmann   Carnegie Mellon University, USA
Riccardo Mariani   Nvidia, Italy
John Molloy   University of York, UK
Fabian Oboril   Intel, Germany
Ganesh Pai   NASA and KBR, USA
Yiannis Papadopoulos   University of Hull, UK
Jan Reich   Fraunhofer IESE, Germany
Selma Saidi   TU Dortmund, Germany
Daniel Schneider   Fraunhofer IESE, Germany
Ran Wei   Dalian University of Technology, China
Michael Woon   Retrospect, USA

Additional Reviewer

Marc Zeller   Siemens, Germany

Case Study Analysis of STPA as Basis for Dynamic Safety Assurance of Autonomous Systems

Laure Buysse[1]([✉])[ID], Dries Vanoost[1][ID], Jens Vankeirsbilck[2][ID],
Jeroen Boydens[2][ID], and Davy Pissoort[1][ID]

[1] Department of Electrical Engineering, Faculty of Engineering Technology,
KU Leuven, Spoorwegstraat 12, 8200 Bruges, Belgium
{laure.buysse,dries.vanoost,davy.pissoort}@kuleuven.be
[2] Department of Computer Science, Faculty of Engineering Technology,
KU Leuven, Spoorwegstraat 12, 8200 Bruges, Belgium
{jens.vankeirsbilck,jeroen.boydens}@kuleuven.be

Abstract. Although in the last decade we have seen a rapid increase in technological and academic developments in the domain of autonomous systems, ensuring the safety of these systems remains extremely challenging. Previously, the concept of dynamic safety cases (DSCs), ConSerts and runtime monitoring frameworks have been presented as an engineering solution for through-life safety assurance. However, these techniques will (initially) be only as good as the claims or rules they hold. Therefore, in this paper we provide a critical view on the use of STPA as a safety and risk analysis technique underlying the design of autonomous systems to aid with the system design and runtime safety assurance. Based on two case studies, we conclude that STPA is a promising technique towards safer autonomous systems. Although hazard generation and modularisation are not easy, we argue that STPA provides a different view on safety which aligns much better with an autonomous system view.

Keywords: STPA · Autonomous systems · Safety analysis

1 Introduction

From industrial robots in factories to autopilot systems and drones in aviation, autonomous systems continue to free us from repetitive, tedious, and monotonous tasks. Over the past decade, significant breakthroughs have been achieved within the domain of autonomous systems with new sophisticated concepts still being introduced every day. Despite these achievements, current safety approaches struggle to handle the ever-increasing complexity of autonomous systems and their often open-ended environments [3,7].

To safely exploit the full potential of autonomous systems, there is a need for a new class of safety techniques which are able to (1) efficiently and fully assess these new technologies, (2) continuously monitor the system through it's

S. Marrone et al. (Eds.): EDCC 2022 Workshops, CCIS 1656, pp. 37–45, 2022.
https://doi.org/10.1007/978-3-031-16245-9_3

life cycle and (3) dynamically update the system and its monitor during runtime [2,5]. To give a few examples, Denney et al. proposed dynamic safety cases (DSCs) as an engineering solution for through-life safety assurance of these complex systems [5]. SMOF, a safety monitoring framework for autonomous systems, developed by Machin et al. takes a different approach and integrates the hazard analysis directly within the framework without making use of safety cases [8]. In [11], Schneider et al. introduce conditional safety certificates (ConSerts), predefined certificates of single (sub-) systems that relate potential safety guarantees with the fulfilment of corresponding environment safety demands which are to be resolved at runtime.

While all these dynamic safety techniques have great potential to significantly improve the safety of autonomous systems, they all still rely on the underlying system safety analysis and the resulting safety requirements. Currently, it is still unclear how to bridge the (static) hazard and risk analysis requirements to meet the new dynamic system assurance techniques [5]. To fill this gap, this paper takes a critical look on the use of Systems-Theoretic Process Analysis (STPA), a systems thinking hazard an risk analysis technique first introduced by Leveson N. and Thomas J. [9].

The remainder of this paper is organised as follows. Section 2 introduces STPA and the underlying STAMP model as well as the connection between STPA and autonomous systems. The use of STPA for autonomous systems and its application to two case studies is discussed within Sect. 3. We provide a breakdown of the acquired safety requirements in Sect. 4. Finally, Sect. 5 presents the conclusion and elaborates on future work.

2   STAMP and STPA

Although dynamic safety cases and safety monitoring frameworks such as SMOF provide a tremendous potential as the next step towards dynamic safety assurance of autonomous systems, it must be acknowledged that these techniques will (initially) be only as good as the claims or rules they hold. Designing and analysing these complex systems with classic safety analysis techniques such as HAZOP or FMEA will most likely not suffice [1,9]. Therefore, this paper considers the use of STAMP, and more specifically, STPA, as a safety and risk analysis technique underlying the design of autonomous systems. The following paragraphs briefly present the theory behind STAMP and STPA and its application to autonomous systems. Using the theory presented here and the practical results discussed in the next session, we aim to answer three fundamental questions:

1. *Complexity* - Can STPA model the complexity which is inherent to autonomous systems? Do we have the ability to represent modular systems, focussing on the complete system or different parts in debt when so desired?
2. *Inclusion* - Is STPA able to handle different operational modes often used within autonomous systems? Does the analysis allow the safety engineer to go beyond the technical questions, including non-safety requirement such as availability and reliability?

3. *Prioritisation* - Is it possible to prioritise certain hazards above others? Can we link faulty system interactions and component failures back to their respective hazards?

System-Theoretic Accident Model and Processes, or STAMP for short, is an accident causality model which is rooted in system thinking and system theory. STAMP looks beyond the chain of directly-related failure events or component failures and includes (more) complex processes and (unsafe) interactions between components. In essence, STAMP reformulates safety as a dynamic control problem, aiming to identify safe and unsafe control actions in the process [9]. As such, it aligns much better with the SUDA-model - Sense the environment and internal state, Understand the environment and internal state, Decide about the next action, Act according to that decision - that forms the base for all autonomous systems (Fig. 1) [10]. Figure 2 shows the concrete mapping of the SUDA-model onto a generic control loop used within STAMP [4].

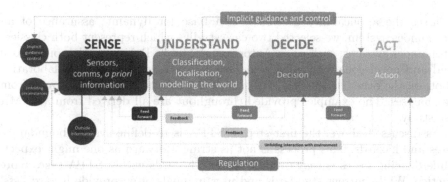

Fig. 1. The basic SUDA model underlying most autonomous systems comprised of four major blocks: "Sense", "Understand", "Decide" and "Act" [10].

Based on the STAMP model, several hazard-and-risk-analysis techniques have been proposed. STPA is one of those techniques, used to proactively analyse a system. At its core, STPA assumes that accidents can be caused by both component failures and unsafe interactions between system components. The analysis itself consist of four steps. Every STPA analysis starts with addressing the fundamental questions behind the analysis such as its purpose, the losses that should be prevented and the system boundaries. Building a model of the system, called a *control structure*, is the second step. Unlike more standard engineering models, the STPA control structures does not capture the physical architecture. Instead, it captures the functional relationships and interactions within the system through a set of feedback control loops. The control actions between loops are analysed in step three. Finally, causal scenarios are derived from the unsafe control actions. Throughout the analysis, safety constraints can be derived at different points [9].

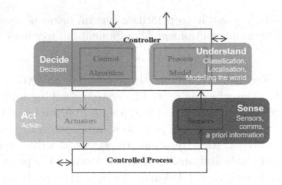

Fig. 2. The SUDA model mapped onto the elements within a generic STAMP control loop.

3   Application and Results

To asses the applicability of STPA as a base for dynamic assurance of an autonomous system, we selected two case studies which represent both classical autonomous systems, such as an Autonomous Mobile Robot (AMR), on the one hand and novel collaborative systems, such as a large industrial collaborative robot, on the other hand. This section will discuss the conclusions drawn from the analyses. The examples provided throughout are all derived from an AMR case study.

As discussed above, the first step of STPA is to define system boundaries, losses and hazards. This process is not as straightforward as one might expect. While defining losses is easy overall, defining hazards within STPA takes more practice. While current standards and user manuals often provide hazard lists, these cannot be used within an STPA analysis due to a definition mismatch. More concretely, current norms such as ISO 12100:2010 [6] define a hazard as *"a potential source of harm"* [6]. STPA on the other hand defines a hazards as *"a system state or set of conditions that, together with a particular set of worst-case environment conditions, will lead to an accident (loss)"* [9].

Thus, defining hazards and losses within STPA requires a different approach, a different way of thinking. Figure 3 illustrates the different approaches applied to the AMR case study. This new way of thinking does introduce some benefits. Not in the least because it allows a safety engineer to include non-safety related losses within the analyses, such as "loss of mission".

For our case studies, we have chosen to focus the analyses on the (autonomous) movement of the systems. These actions are not only the most hazardous, but often involve complex algorithms, calculations and a myriad of sensory information (both for safety and correct navigation). The ability to focus on different tasks of the system or analyse the system at a more abstract or detailed level is one of the major benefits of using STPA for these complex systems. Through the use of control structures as defined in step two of STPA, the safety engineer is free to decide how detailed or abstract an analysis should be

Hazard according to ISO 12100:2010	Hazard within STPA
Moving elements	Violation of minimum separation rules between the AMR/infrastructure/humans/animals
Falling objects	Equipment under unnecessary stress

Fig. 3. Comparison between example hazards as defined in ISO 12100:2010 (Safety of Machinery - General principles for design - Risk assessment and risk reduction) [6] and hazards as defined within STPA [9].

at any point, with the ability to focus on one control loop at a time. Special care does need to be taken when designing the control structure. The control structure is not just any system (hardware) model as is often used within a standard design process. Rather, it defines control loops and is based more on system tasks, functionality and feedback signals.

Generating unsafe control actions (UCAs), step three of the analysis, is done through analysing each control action (CA) within each control loop. STPA defines four categories of UCAs:

1. *Not Provided*: CAs not provided when they are needed.
2. *Provided*: CAs provided when not necessary.
3. *Timing*: CAs provided too late, too early or in the wrong order.
4. *Duration*: CAs provided too long or too short. This category can only occur if the control action is represented using a continuous signal. It goes without saying that discrete signals can never fall within this category.

For complex systems, this step is quite daunting due to sheer size of the system and the amount of possible issues. We propose to use a hierarchical context list (HCL) to help solve this problem. A main context list is used to define status or system specific contexts. Sub-lists are then created for each task. If so desired, separate lower-level lists can also be made for each controller. Figure 4 provides a partial example structure. Formally defining context lists not only helps to ensure all scenarios are accounted for, but they help declutter the analysis and introduce modularity, aiding the addition of dynamic safety assurance in later stages. Using the context list, system changes can be made more easily without having the revisit and redo the entire analysis.

Of course, each generated action has to be analysed and categorised as 'safe' (a desired system state) or 'unsafe' (unsafe state - possible issue). It is worth noting that within all case studies, the STPA analysis discovered (subtle) design flaws, which were unknown till then. We highlight two issues found with the AMR:

1. *UCA: The driving controller of the AMR halts the AMR while its driving on a ramp.*

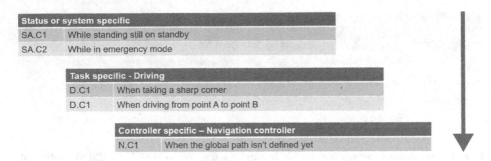

Fig. 4. Example of a hierarchical list of context tables for an autonomous mobile robot

While stopping the AMR is generally no issue, the AMR always brakes using its motor as it has not actual brakes. For steep descends or inclines, this might pose some interesting challenges to the AMR. Moreover, breaking on the motor could decrease the lifespan of the system and it is impossible to guarantee the system will be able to stop at all times.

2. *UCA: The driving controller does not let the AMR drive backwards when there is no other way out.*

   While driving and delivering packages, is possible for the AMR to get cornered on three sides. The preferable course of action would be to drive backwards and then continue the mission without any human intervention. However, the mobile robot does not have any LIDAR at the back. This makes driving backwards a risky endeavour, initially prohibited and assumed to be unnecessary at all times.

The final step of STPA is to derive causal scenarios. While this step is extremely important for the final results, this step is also the most unstructured. Generally speaking, causal scenarios are defined within four main categories:

1. Unsafe controller behaviour
2. Inadequate feedback/data/information
3. Control path issues
4. Faults within the control process factors

For all case studies, using these categories turned out to be insufficient, leaving the final analysis cluttered, impossible to update and generally unstructured. Changes to a system ended up difficult or impossible as we could no longer trace back the causal scenarios (and associated safety requirements) to the right controller or process. To analyse complex systems and retain traceability, we recommend to analyse each controller separately using multiple tables. These tables can be further divided based on the control actions.

4   Requirement Analysis

At the end of a successful STPA analysis, a large amount of data has been generated in the form of unsafe actions and (safety) requirements and constraints. We identify three points within an STPA analysis where safety requirements need to be defined: (1) high-level safety requirements based on the hazard list, (2) requirements based on the unsafe causal actions and (3) requirements based on the causal scenarios.

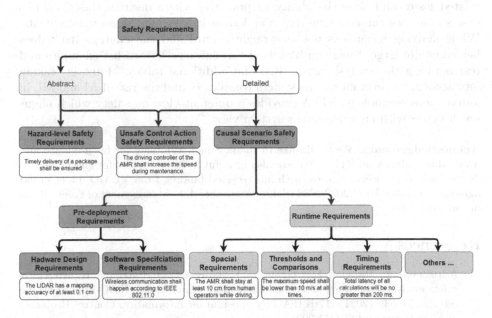

Fig. 5. Breakdown of STPA requirements

The high-level safety requirements within STPA are very abstract. They should primarily be used for early design decisions and general safety considerations. In comparison, UCA requirements are far less abstract, focussing on only one action and one control loop. However, UCA requirements can still encompass multiple components of the system as one control loop does not necessarily match with one system component. The requirements generated at the end of the STPA analysis, CS requirements, are the most detailed of all. They often talk about smaller details, singular components or specific parts of the communication chain, thus making them perfect for dynamic system assurance. CS constraints are most likely to contain concrete system thresholds, ideal for runtime monitoring. It needs to be said that CS requirements come in multiple different types, not all suited for runtime assurance. Some CS requirements define detailed hardware requirements or software requirements, such as the use of a specific chip to meet measurements thresholds or the use of a specific algorithm to process data. These types of requirements are inherently not runtime requirements. Figure 5 features all identified categories, supplemented with examples from the AMR case study.

5   Conclusion

In this paper, we studied the use of STPA to analyse complex autonomous systems and generate the required safety constraints. We posed that the analysis should be able to deal with complexity, allow for the inclusion of non-safety related losses and have the ability to prioritize where desired. Based on two case studies, we can conclude that STPA does indeed fulfil these requirements. While deriving hazards is not as straightforward and the analysis itself does become quite large, these can be solved through new hazard list examples and restructuring the analysis using HCL and additional tables. Moreover, taking into account the ever increasing system complexity and the rise of AI and ML in autonomous technology, STPA provides a different view on safety which aligns much better with an autonomous system view.

Acknowledgements. We would like to thank Simon Whiteley for his guidance and invaluable feedback on STPA. We are also grateful to M. Conradie for the numerous discussions on the work. The research has received funding from VLAIO under grand agreement number HBC.2020.2088 (Safety Assurance 4.0 - Management of Safety Risks in Industry 4.0).

References

1. Adriaensen, A., Pintelon, L., Costantino, F., Gravio, G.D., Patriarca, R.: An STPA safety analysis case study of a collaborative robot application. IFAC-PapersOnLine **54**(1), 534–539 (2021). 17th IFAC Symposium on Information Control Problems in Manufacturing INCOM 2021
2. Asaadi, E., Denney, E., Menzies, J., Pai, G.J., Petroff, D.: Dynamic assurance cases: a pathway to trusted autonomy. Computer **53**(12), 35–46 (2020). https://doi.org/10.1109/MC.2020.3022030
3. Burton, S., Habli, I., Lawton, T., McDermid, J., Morgan, P., Porter, Z.: Mind the gaps: assuring the safety of autonomous systems from an engineering, ethical, and legal perspective. Artif. Intell. **279**, 103201 (2020). https://doi.org/10.1016/j.artint.2019.103201
4. Buysse, L., Conradie, M., Vanoost, D., Pissoort, D.: STPA and autonomy: fries or foes? A case study analysis. In: MIT STAMP Workshop (2022). http://psas.scripts.mit.edu/home/2022-stamp-workshop-program/
5. Denney, E., Pai, G., Habli, I.: Dynamic safety cases for through-life safety assurance. In: 37th International Conference on Software Engineering, pp. 1–4, May 2015
6. International Organization for Standardization: ISO 12100:2010: Safety of machinery - General principles for design - Risk assessment and risk reduction. International Organisation for Standardization (2010)
7. Javed, M.A., Muram, F.U., Hansson, H., Punnekkat, S., Thane, H.: Towards dynamic safety assurance for industry 4.0. J. Syst. Archit. **114**, 101914 (2021). https://doi.org/10.1016/j.sysarc.2020.101914

8. Machin, M., Guiochet, J., Waeselynck, H., Blanquart, J.P., Roy, M., Masson, L.: SmoF - a safety monitoring framework for autonomous systems. IEEE Trans. Syst. Man Cybern. Syst. **48**(5), 702–715 (2018). https://doi.org/10.1109/TSMC.2016. 2633291. https://hal.archives-ouvertes.fr/hal-01394139

9. Nancy, L., John, T.: STPA Handbook. MIT Partnership for Systems Approaches to Safety and Security (PSASS), March 2018

10. Nicholson, M., Hawkins, R., Johnson, N.: Workshop on autonomy and AI. In: Safety Critical Systems Symposium (2019)

11. Schneider, D., Trapp, M.: Engineering conditional safety certificates for open adaptive systems. IFAC Proc. Vol. **46**(22), 139–144 (2013). https://doi. org/10.3182/20130904-3-UK-4041.00037. https://www.sciencedirect.com/science/ article/pii/S1474667015340015. 4th IFAC Workshop on Dependable Control of Discrete Systems

Continuous, Systematic Risk Mapping of Roads as an Input for Dynamic Risk Management (DRM) in Autonomous Systems

Arno Wolter[1], Michaela Grahl[1(✉)], and Jörg Ehlers[2]

[1] Initiative für sichere Straßen GmbH, Matthias-Grünewald-Str. 1-3, 53175 Bonn, Germany
{a.wolter,m.grahl}@sichere-strassen.org
[2] Institute of Highway Engineering, RWTH Aachen University, Mies-van-der-Rohe-Str. 1, 52074 Aachen, Germany
ehlers@isac.rwth-aachen.de

Abstract. The risk potential on German roads remains high: Even in 2021 with less traffic due to the Covid-pandemic, the police counted 2.3 million traffic accidents [1]. Many accidents occur due to individual mistakes of road users. Dangerous situations are often misjudged or not recognized on time, for example, due to distraction while driving [2]. Autonomous systems in vehicles show the potential to avoid driver-related accidents, but for a Dynamic Risk Management (DRM) reliable data is needed. This is exactly where the project "Early Detection of Dangerous Areas in road traffic using smart data - EDDA+" comes in. The road hazard map created by using the EDDA+ method evaluates the Germany-wide road network according to a hazard score. This digital, safety-related data includes a lot of contextual information like weather or daytime conditions and can be used as an additional basis for the DRM risk analysis. For example, an autonomous system could react more sensitively at road areas where the hazard score is high. This continuously updated hazard map is published on www.gefahrenstellen.de and also available in a more detailed way on our platform for professional users such as local authorities, police, science, engineering offices, navigation providers and car manufacturers.

Keywords: Hazard map · Road safety · Risk analysis

1 Germany-Wide EDDA+ Road Hazard Map - Data Sources and Method of Calculation

The identification and verification of danger spots occurs mainly through the aggregation and analysis of data from three different data sources (see Fig. 1).

The first data source is collision data, which is collected by the police authorities via their IT systems. It is already actively used for road safety work, such as accident type maps for the work of the road safety commissions. This data source has the disadvantage

S. Marrone et al. (Eds.): EDCC 2022 Workshops, CCIS 1656, pp. 46–53, 2022.
https://doi.org/10.1007/978-3-031-16245-9_4

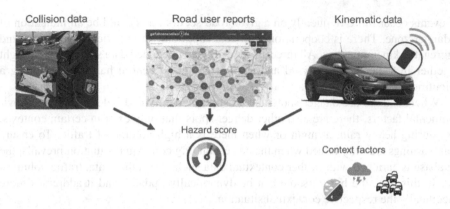

Fig. 1. Scheme of data sources and EDDA+ approach

that it follows a reactive approach looking at danger spots after the fact. Consequently, several accidents must have already occurred over a longer period of time for a danger spot to appear as an accident black spot in the analysis. In order to do justice to a more proactive early detection of danger spots, two new data sources have been added as part of the EDDA+ framework: reports from road users as well as kinematic data generated from cars and smartphones.

For the collection of road user reports, the platform and app gefahrenstellen.de (dangerspots.org) was developed, which allows road users from all over Germany to report and comment danger zones on a map thus taking advantage of a systematic crowdsourcing approach. When the reports are submitted by the users, automated prompts are made to describe the danger spot in more detail and to indicate for whom this spot is dangerous (e.g. pedestrians, cyclists and/or motorised drivers). For precise geocoding, pins can be inserted on the entire German road network (in urban and rural areas as well as on highways). The focus is on danger spots where risky situations arise on a regular basis due to poor or unclear road conditions, misbehaviour of road users or certain weather constellations.

The proactive reports of road users can be used to make near-crashes and minor crashes visible which have not been reported to the police and which could indicate a potential new accident blackspot. The results from the successful pilot phase in the German cities of Aachen and Bonn have shown that, on the one hand, these reports confirm already known accident blackspots. On the other hand, they also reveal danger spots that were not previously known. In the analysis, not only the information from the report itself, but also the number of supporters of a report as well as the user comments and pictures were identified as important parameters. Within 6 months, 3,500 road user reports pertaining to 1,500 danger spots were collected in Aachen and Bonn during the pilot phase [3–5]. Thanks to continuous press releases, there are currently reports on more than 7000 danger spots throughout Germany, with thousands of supporters.

In the context of the project, kinematic data refers to safety-critical movement data from cars and smartphones that could indicate a dangerous situation. Examples of safety-critical movements are harsh braking or evasive manoeuvres. If such driving manoeuvres or events occur more frequently on a given road section, this could be an indication of a danger zone. There is cooperation with data suppliers who provide anonymised and aggregated kinematic data. All three aforementioned geocoded data sources are brought together in a database, analysed and aggregated into a central hazard score using a scientifically based algorithm.

Whereas there are danger spots that exist permanently and independently of environmental factors, there are also other danger spots that only exist in certain contexts, e.g. during heavy rain, at night or when there is a high volume of traffic. To ensure that warnings are only issued when the corresponding contextual situation prevails, the database is enriched with further contextual data such as weather data, traffic volumes, etc. In this way, the hazard score can be dynamically updated and it addresses more specifically the respective contextual situation.

As a basic feature of the EDDA+ project, the previously determined hazard scores are displayed on a Germany-wide road hazard map. It contains an aggregated, dynamic hazard score for the entire road network in Germany, in urban and rural areas as well as on highways.

To ensure a clear and intuitive presentation, the calculation and display of the hazard score is based on predefined road segments. For this purpose, the road network was divided into individual segments using a new method taking into account the characteristics of junctions and sections. The method was optimised primarily for the special features of a dense road network with many traffic nodes, as is the case in urban environments. However, this segmentation is also applicable to other non-urban areas, such as rural roads and highways. For the calculation of the hazard score, the data is blended together into a safety score for each segment of the road network. This comprises two steps. First, a baseline safety score is calculated based on accident data and safety critical driving manoeuvers. In order to take into account the relationships between accidents and safety critical driving manoeuvres at neighbouring segments, these point events are smoothed over several segments, whereby events closer together are given more weight than events further away. In the second step, user reports on dangerous spots enhance the hazard score for regions where the data is available. The resulting hazard score thus combines a reactive and proactive perspective to further enhance current traffic safety work.

The road hazard map (see Fig. 2) contains an extensive filter and analysis tool so that the display of danger spots can be individually adapted to the relevant question or application of the user. As such different views and filters can be selected e.g. by type of road user, by type of road, type of hazard, and many more. Likewise, weather-related or traffic volume-related danger spots can be filtered.

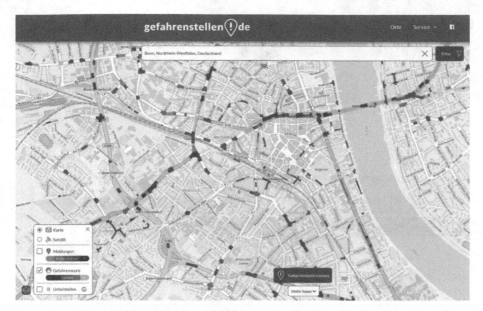

Fig. 2. EDDA+ road hazard map on gefahrenstellen.de

2 Data Usage for EDDA+ Road Hazard Map

The data from the road hazard map can be individually processed and incorporated into both, existing as well as new applications, such as apps, navigation services, advanced driver assistance systems, websites/platforms, analysis or application software. Through a survey, the following user groups have emerged as the most relevant for the EDDA+ information: Science/universities, local authorities, engineering offices, police, industry (OEMs and their suppliers, navigation services, insurance, fleet management) and road users. In the next section of this paper, we would like to discuss concrete use cases for autonomous driving and further use cases for the user groups "road users/industry" and "local authorities/police" (see Fig. 3).

2.1 Use Cases for Autonomous Driving

In the future, (partially) autonomous driving will play an increasingly important role. Detailed insights and reliable digital data on existing or potential danger spots are therefore also particularly important for car manufacturers and suppliers. Live data on short-term danger spots such as the end of a traffic jam or objects on the road can be played out as warnings via connected driving systems. However, structural danger spots with a longer-term character cannot yet be depicted through such systems. In such cases, the EDDA+ information can be fed into the vehicle's systems before the journey and linked to the sensor data of the vehicle. E.g. in case of limited visibility, the driver can be warned accordingly or certain vehicle devices or functionalities can be triggered automatically (such as switching on a night light assistant). Since the EDDA+ database is available

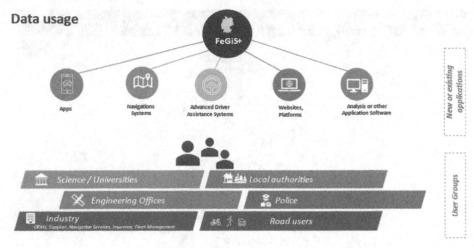

Fig. 3. Data usage and user group

offline, the road hazard map can generally be used as a redundant system in case of network failure or gaps.

Furthermore, this digital, safety-related data includes a lot of contextual information like weather or daytime conditions and can be used as an additional basis for the DRM risk analysis. For example, an autonomous system could react more sensitively at road areas where the hazard score is high.

2.2   Further Use Cases for Road Users and Industry

In many road crashes, the misbehaviour or inappropriate driving-style of road users is a frequent cause of accidents. Within the framework of EDDA+, user-friendly applications are to be created to help road users to drive carefully at danger points. Furthermore, the information from the digital road hazard map will be processed in such a way that it can be incorporated into existing applications from other third-party providers (navigation systems, telematic systems, fleet management) and advanced driver-assistance systems (ADAS). Various functions can be derived from the hazard map. In the following, we would like to present some of these functions as examples (see Fig. 4).

Excessive or inappropriate speed represents a misbehaviour of road users that often leads to collisions on certain road sections. These road sections can be identified via the EDDA+ database and linked to a warning system. If the driving style is inappropriate while passing such a high score danger spot, an intuitive, dynamic warning alerts the driver to reduce speed. In order to avoid an excessive or even disturbing number of alerts, these can be customized according to the driver's preferences and personal profile. The system could also use the driving style and its contextualization as an indicator by issuing a warning sound, only if the speed is inappropriate in relation to the location and its context. In that instance, the system would remain silent most of the time and would only intervene, when the driver misjudges the situation/risk level at the current position.

USE CASES
early warnings / driver assistance

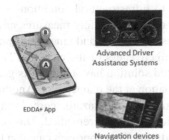

Advanced Driver Assistance Systems

EDDA+ App

Navigation devices

- Intuitive, dynamic **warnings** according to hazard score at danger spots (e.g. acceptable or inappropriate driving behaviour)

- **Suspend** distracting (smartphone-) **notifications** in dangerous areas with higher risk levels

- Investigating **safer routes** for e.g. cyclists, pedestrians / safest way to school

- Autonomous driving: data input for risk analysis (Dynamic Risk Management)

- Apps for **high risk groups:** young drivers, elderly drivers

- **Safety analysis** of aggregated and anonymized data for fleet management

Fig. 4. User cases for road users and industry

In recent years, distracted driving, especially through the use of smartphones, has often led to accidents. In dangerous areas with higher risk levels such distracting smartphone messages or functionalities could be temporarily disabled. The platform and app offer vulnerable road users, such as cyclists and pedestrians, the opportunity to find out about dangerous areas in their region and to select safer routes. Parents in particular can thus determine a safer route to school for their children. The information on danger zones can also be integrated into existing navigation and routing systems in order to display the safest route in addition to the existing routing options for the fastest and shortest route.

Numerous road safety projects focus on high-risk groups within society that represent particularly vulnerable road users. These include e.g. children, novice drivers and senior citizens. Each risk group presents an individual challenge for road safety work. These individual requirements can be taken into account in the context of an app development and special app-variations or functionalities can be tailored to the needs of each risk group.

With regard to fleet vehicles, road safety analyses on fleet drivers are only possible to a very limited extent for data protection reasons. Through the development of a special fleet tool, aggregated and anonymised safety analyses of a fleet can be offered on the company-independent platform gefahrenstellen.de on a supra-regional or regional basis.

2.3 Use Cases for Local Authorities and the Police

The EDDA+ analysis tools can also be narrowed down to regional areas. This means that the information on danger sports can be made available to municipalities and police authorities as an additional source of analysis for the road safety work in their region. By combining collision data with user-feedback and kinematic data, geocoded danger spots can be identified at an early stage before the area develops into a collision black spot. With regard to existing collision blackspots, the user-feedback and kinematic data provide valuable information that can be used to decide on appropriate measures. For example, the comments of the users regarding the danger spots can be used to analyse the viewpoint of the road users and thus provide a new perspective on the danger spot.

Furthermore, by identifying risky driving manoeuvres on a road section the kinematic data can provide critical insights with regards to infrastructural conditions and potential challenges. After construction measures or other road safety measures have been implemented, the two proactive indicators (i.e. user-feedback and kinematic data) represent an important new evaluation tool for the effectiveness of the changes. This ensures a better and swifter control, if the implemented solution has achieved its goal or has caused no change or even has worsened the situation at the danger spot. Another aspect is that a prioritisation of danger points is possible via the hazard score. In this way, the particularly urgent hot spots can be quickly identified and remedied. This prioritisation can also be used to target municipal expenditure. This approach can also be presented transparently to the local citizens.

In general, the desire for citizen participation is growing nowadays, especially with regards to municipal transport issues. The municipalities are already receiving many enquiries on the subject of danger spots from local citizens. The gefahrenstellen.de platform offers municipalities a central forum where they can enter into a dialogue with their citizens on topics relevant to traffic safety. On the city sub-pages on gefahrenstellen.de set up for this purpose, the municipality can comment on the danger spot hotspots in its region and present already planned structural measures in road traffic. In this way, previous enquiries can be channelled centrally and answered more effectively. In addition, a feature is already offered with which municipalities can motivate their citizens to submit hazard reports. Via the additional feature, these hazard reports can be specifically attributed to predefined used-groups and can be evaluated separately. With the help of the EDDA+ analysis tool "Pro-Portal", police and local authorities can define places where they can increase the awareness of road users to dangerous situations e.g. through increased police presence at the danger spots.

2.4 Current Developments of EDDA+

For local authorities and the police, a login area and advanced PRO version has been developed as pro.gefahrenstellen.de. Authorised registered users have access to sophisticated analysis and filter tools. All data and its representation can be customized according to the needs and desired time periods. This PRO version (Fig. 5) is available since the beginning of this year.

The hazard score map is currently available for 10 of 16 German federal states and published on gefahrenstellen.de. The remaining states will follow by summer 2022. From the second half of this year an extension of the EDDA+ approach to other European countries is planned.

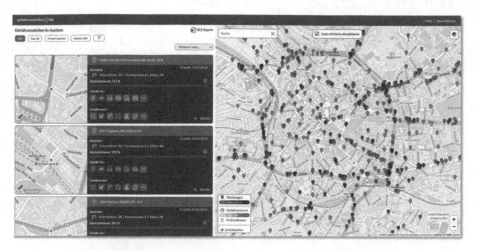

Fig. 5. Screenshot of EDDA+ analysis tool Pro-Portal

3 Project Partners

The EDDA+ project consortium consists of the Initiative for Safer Roads, the RWTH Aachen University (Institute of Highway Engineering), the German Police University (Transport Studies & Traffic Psychology), PTV Planung Transport Verkehr AG and DTV-Verkehrsconsult GmbH.

The project period spans from 1st July 2019 to 30th September 2022. EDDA+ is co-funded by the German Federal Ministry for Digital and Transport (BMDV). gefahrenstellen.de will be continued after the project period by Initiative for Safer Roads.

References

1. Federal Statistical Office (Destatis), Road traffic accidents in 2021. https://www.destatis.de/EN/Themes/Society-Environment/Traffic-Accidents/Tables/accidents-registered-police.html
2. German Road Safety Council, Annual report 2019. https://www.dvr.de/fileadmin/downloads/dvr-jahresbericht/DVR-Jahresbericht-2019.pdf
3. Initiative for Safer Roads, RWTH Aachen University (2019). FeGiS – Früherkennung von Gefahrenstellen im Straßenverkehr: Final report. Leibniz Information Centre for Science and Technology University Library. https://www.tib.eu/en/search/id/TIBKAT:1679013440?cHash=a8668d6b0973b2ccc61274f87cccb42a
4. German Federal Ministry of Digital and Transport, Project description and results of FeGiS. https://www.bmvi.de/SharedDocs/DE/Artikel/DG/mfund-projekte/frueherkennung-von-gefahrenstellen-im-strassenverkehr-fegis.html
5. Offermanns, H.: Online users identify 250 danger spots in Aachen. Aachener Nachrichten (Print) (2019). https://www.aachener-nachrichten.de/lokales/aachen/die-resonanz-auf-das-projekt-gefahrenstellende-ist-in-aachen-gross_aid-37696875

Workshop on Artificial Intelligence for RAILwayS (AI4RAILS)

Workshop on Artificial Intelligence
for RAILwayS (AI4RAILS)

Workshop Description

AI4RAILS 2022 was the third edition in an international workshop series specifically addressing topics related to the adoption of artificial intelligence (AI) in the railway domain. In the last few years, there has been a growing interest in AI applications to railway systems. Such interest has been a consequence of the potential and opportunities enabled by AI-powered solutions in combination with the other prominent technologies based on cloud computing, big data analytics, and the Internet of Things. The results already achieved in other relevant transport sectors, mainly automotive, have further supported the development of AI in railways. This trend within the railway industry is also witnessed by the industrial research and innovation initiatives as well as by the growing number of scientific publications addressing AI techniques applied to the rail sector. Relevant applications include intelligent surveillance, automatic train operation, smart maintenance, timetable optimization, and network management.

The application of AI to railways is expected to have a significant impact in a medium to long term perspective, especially within autonomous and cooperative driving, predictive maintenance, and traffic management optimization. For example, railway lines capacity, life cycle cost (LCC), human errors detection and avoidance, efficiency and performance, automation, and self-adaptation, among other things, could significantly benefit from artificial intelligence and machine learning. This opens unprecedented scenarios for railway systems, but also raises concerns regarding system dependability and the new threats associated with a higher level of autonomy. Therefore, one of the first steps towards the adoption of AI in the railway sector is understanding to what extent AI can be considered reliable, safe, and secure (i.e., what is sometimes referred to as "trustworthy AI", including "explainable AI") given the peculiarities and reference standards of the railway domain. At the same time, it is extremely relevant to understand to what extent AI can help achieve higher levels of reliability, safety, and security within the railway domain. We can summarize these two opposite yet strictly interconnected aspects as "dependable AI for smarter railways" and "AI for more dependable railways"; hence, the connection between AI4RAILS and the hosting European Dependable Computing Conference (EDCC).

The AI challenge has been tackled by the European Union's Shift2Rail program with several research and innovation projects addressing aspects of digitalization, automation, and optimization. In particular, the aim of the ongoing Shift2Rail project named RAILS (Roadmaps for AI integration in the raiL Sector) is to investigate the potential of AI in the rail sector and contribute to the definition of roadmaps for future research in next-generation signalling systems, operational intelligence, and network management. This workshop is part of the dissemination activities planned in the RAILS project.

The ambition of AI4RAILS is to be a reference forum for researchers, practitioners, and business leaders to discuss and share new perspectives, ideas, technologies, experience, and solutions for effective and dependable integration of AI techniques in rail-based transportation systems, in the general context of intelligent and smart railways.

The format of this year's edition of AI4RAILS included two keynotes and three technical sessions. The first keynote speech was given by Christian Chavanel, Director of Rail System at International Union of Railways (UIC, France). The speech described the state of play and the perspectives for the implementation of AI in the European railway sector, also describing how AI technologies are currently deployed in the railway sector and how they should be in the future, with examples concerning face recognition in the fight against terrorism, chatbots and virtual assistants for passengers, predictive maintenance, and other real-case scenarios. The second keynote speech was given by The MathWorks, a worldwide leading company in the fields of data science and machine learning platforms, as recognized by the Gartner's Magic Quadrant 2020, mainly known for their Matlab and Simulink software applications. We received many quality submissions by contributors from seven distinct countries. Each paper was reviewed by at least three reviewers from diverse institutions and nations, including reputable academic and industry representatives. After the blind peer-review process, we finally selected seven papers for presentation at the workshop and publication in the book of proceedings. The review process focused on the originality of the papers, significance, relevance, and clarity of presentation. The acceptance/rejection decision on the papers was a result of the independent reviewers' opinions, final discussion, and agreement. The papers presented in this edition represent an interesting blend of approaches and techniques addressing several challenges in the application of AI to railways, such as scheduling and train control, monitoring and maintenance, and data analysis.

The organization of this workshop was supported by the aforementioned Shift2Rail project named RAILS. RAILS has received funding from the European Union's Horizon 2020 research and innovation program under grant agreement no. 881782.

We would like to thank the keynote speakers and the international members of the Technical Program Committee for kindly accepting our invitations. We are very grateful to them and to all workshop speakers for their outstanding contributions, which also made this edition of AI4RAILS a success, exceeding our expectations. We also thank all the people who supported this workshop and helped us in its organization, including the EDCC chairs and organizers.

Organization

Workshop Chairs and Organizers

Stefano Marrone — University of Naples Federico II, Italy
Roberto Nardone — University of Naples Parthenope, Italy

Steering Committee

Valeria Vittorini — University of Naples Federico II, Italy
Francesco Flammini — Mälardalen University and Linnaeus University, Sweden
Rob Goverde — TU Delft, The Netherlands
Ronghui Liu — University of Leeds, UK

Technical Program Committee

Davide Barbato — Hitachi Rail STS, Italy
Nikola Bešinović — Delft University of Technology, The Netherlands
Lorenzo De Donato — University of Naples Federico II, Italy
Francesco Flammini — Mälardalen University and Linnaeus University, Sweden
Rob Goverde — Delft University of Technology, The Netherlands
Fredrik Heintz — Linköping University, Sweden
Zhiyuan Lin — University of Leeds, UK
Stefano Marrone — University of Naples Federico II, Italy
Claudio Mazzariello — Hitachi Rail STS, Italy
Roberto Nardone — University of Naples Parthenope, Italy
Alberto Petrillo — University of Naples Federico II, Italy
Danijela Ristic-Durrant — University of Bremen, Germany
Carlo Sansone — University of Naples Federico II, Italy
Stefania Santini — University of Naples Federico II, Italy
Ruifan Tang — University of Leeds, UK
Valeria Vittorini — University of Naples Federico II, Italy

A Literature Review for the Application of Artificial Intelligence in the Maintenance of Railway Operations with an Emphasis on Data

Mauro José Pappaterra(✉) (iD)

Department of Computer Science, Uppsala University, Uppsala, Sweden
mauro.pappaterra@ieee.com

Abstract. This literature review aims for a holistic overview of Artificial Intelligence (AI) applications in the railway industry. Our research covers specifically the subdomain of railway maintenance. We have analyzed the state of the art of AI applied to the railway industry by conducting an extensive literature review, summarizing different tasks and problems belonging to railway maintenance and common AI-based models implemented for their solution. Within this study we present an integrated overview with special emphasis on the data used to create these models.

The results of our research show that the possible applications of AI for the maintenance of railway operations are vast and there are many problems and tasks that can greatly benefit from it. Moreover, very different types of data are implemented to feed AI models: including not only numerical, text and image data but a wide variety of data types ranging from sound, GPS coordinates, track geometry, speed and acceleration data, data from rolling stock vibrations, knowledge from experts, historical data from logs and reports, temperature data and more. Data can also be harvested using different technologies such as IoT devices, wireless networks, smart sensors, computer-based simulations, and digital twins. These and more insights are discussed in detail within this paper.

Keywords: Railways · Maintenance · Artificial Intelligence · Literature review · Open datasets

1 Introduction

The increasing number of IoT devices, data available and computer power (along with the decreasing manufacturing costs for technology) create promising conditions for the application of modern AI techniques in the railway sector.

We have consulted several literature reviews on specific AI applications in the railway industry. Some reviews contemplate different railway subdomains, including not only maintenance but also safety and security, traffic planning, scheduling, logistics, optimization and more [1, 2]. Other studies focus on very specific maintenance applications and AI methodologies. For instance, different authors have surveyed the literature on Machine Learning applications for track maintenance [3] and detection of wheel defects [4]; the study [5] presents an overview on fault detection in railway switch and crossing systems; other authors [6] investigated image processing approaches for track inspection; a recent study [7] presents a survey on the utilization of Deep Learning and audio and video sensors for railway maintenance.

This literature review aims for a holistic overview of AI applications in railway systems. We cover both traditional AI models and more numerical-based black-box approaches. The first approach refers to symbolic AI, systems that mimic human intelligence by resorting to rules and AI ontologies related to a particular domain that are transcribed into computer algorithms. In contrast, numerical-based Machine Learning models (such as Artificial Neural Networks) can be extremely complex and have thousands of layers and parameters. This inherent complexity is defined as black-box AI [1]. Our research considers both symbolic and black-box AI and covers specifically the subdomain of railway maintenance. Including papers related to the preservation, inspection, maintenance and monitoring of railway tracks, assets, infrastructure, and rolling stock. Our previous research revealed that the amount of publicly available datasets specific to AI applications in the railway industry have increased over the past years. We have also identified a good number of readily available open datasets that can be implemented in research problems related to the application of AI for the maintenance of railway systems [8]. In contrast with the existing literature, this research puts a special emphasis on data utilized to feed these AI models.

2 Methodology

For this literature review a wide variety of papers on the subject of AI applied to the maintenance of railway systems were consulted. The portals used for the search include: ResearchGate, Google Scholar, IEEE Xplore Digital Library, SpringerLink, ACM Digital Library, ScienceDirect and Elsevier Scopus. These sources are briefly described in Table 1.

The search terms used to find the papers are a combination of the following key words: AI, railway, artificial intelligence, railway industry, machine learning, maintenance, predictive maintenance, condition-based maintenance, corrective maintenance, fault detection and diagnosis, and fault prognosis. These keywords were combined alternately in different order. The searches were performed from April to mid-September 2021.

For the selection of papers, the study main content needed to be centered on the application of AI methods to solve any railway task related to maintenance. For the scope of this review, the range of the years of publication was set from 1990 to 2020. Papers that presented better quality (relevant content, clear methodology, critical analysis, reproducibility, sound interpretation and documentation, innovative ideas, etc.) were prioritized over papers of inferior characteristics. So is the case for papers that were more referenced from reputable sources or were published in creditable journals. After applying this inclusion/exclusion criteria we collected a total of 57 papers from approximately ~200 papers. Many papers were excluded because they were not presenting an AI-based solution, they were not centered in maintenance or simply did not pass our aforementioned criteria in any other way.

Table 1. Search portals consulted for the collection of literature.

Search portal	Short description	URL
ACM Digital Library	An academic research platform from the Association for Computing Machinery (ACM)	https://dl.acm.org/
Elsevier Scopus	Elsevier's abstract and citation database curated by experts in different fields	https://www.scopus.com/
Google Scholar	Google's search engine for scholarly literature	https://scholar.google.com/
IEEE Xplore Digital Library	IEEE's research database for academic publications	https://ieeexplore.ieee.org/
ResearchGate	European platform for academic research and networking	https://www.researchgate.net/
ScienceDirect	Elsevier's database of scientific publications	https://www.sciencedirect.com/
SpringerLink	Search platform for Springer academic publications	https://link.springer.com/

3 Literature Review

This section includes the complete literature review. The full list of papers that have been examined can be found in the *References* section.

3.1 Papers Overview

The maintenance and monitoring of railway infrastructure and assets are vital to the railway industry. We have identified a total of 57 papers on the application of AI within this domain. The following subdomains were elicited based on the classification of the papers: railway tracks maintenance, rolling stock maintenance, railway infrastructure maintenance, monitoring, and maintenance planning. Notice that the scope of some papers can cover more than one of the subdomains described. Figure 1 presents the papers divided by year of publication; Table 2 displays the list of maintenance applications and the AI approaches identified; and Table 3 displays the types of data found in the literature.

3.2 Papers Review

The review of the selected papers is presented below. The papers are divided in subsections according to the classification presented in Sect. 3.1.

Railway Tracks Maintenance. One of the big tasks within the domain is the maintenance of the railway tracks and their parts. Some studies propose solutions based on Deep Learning (DL). For instance, authors in [9] propose the implementation of DL

Table 2. Papers from the literature review divided by railway maintenance application.

Railway maintenance application	AI solution approach	Citations
Railway tracks maintenance	Artificial neural networks	[9–15, 17–20, 26, 27, 29]
	Computer vision	[9, 19, 29]
	Data mining	[10, 11, 16, 17, 21, 23–25]
	Fuzzy logic	[22]
	Knowledge-based systems	[28]
Rolling stock maintenance	Artificial neural networks	[32, 34, 37, 41, 46]
	Computer vision	[30, 33, 38, 39]
	Data mining	[31, 35, 36, 40, 42, 43, 45, 46]
	Fuzzy logic	[22]
	Genetic algorithms	[38, 39]
	Isolation forest	[46]
	Particle swarm optimization	[37, 41]
Infrastructure maintenance	Artificial neural networks	[47, 49, 51, 54]
	Bayesian networks	[52]
	Computer vision	[47, 48, 53]
	Data mining	[21, 50, 55, 56, 61]
	Fuzzy logic	[49]
	Genetic algorithms	[55]
Monitoring	Agent theory	[57]
	Artificial neural networks	[19, 27, 51]
	Bayesian networks	[52]
	Computer vision	[19]
	Data mining	[19, 21, 45, 50, 59–61]
	Fuzzy logic	[62]
	Stochastic models	[58]
Maintenance planning	Bayesian networks	[63]
	Fuzzy logic	[64]
	Heuristics	[65]
	Support vector machines	[63]

along with image processing for fault detection (FD) in railway track fasteners. The implementation relies on image detection, feature extraction and a classifier algorithm. A different approach [10] implements DL and AdaBoost algorithms for detecting broken fasteners. More than 4000 images were used to create this model. This study presents a

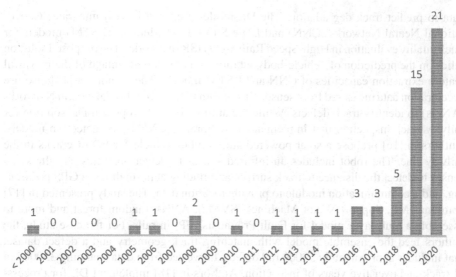

Fig. 1. Number of papers in the literature review divided by year of publication.

Table 3. Papers from the literature review divided by type of data implemented.

Type of data	Citations
Acoustic and sound data	[16, 31, 45, 46]
GPS coordinates and location	[16, 28, 34, 44, 45, 65]
Image and video	[9, 10, 19, 22, 29, 30, 32–34, 38, 39, 47, 48, 53, 54]
Knowledge from experts	[24, 26, 35, 49, 58]
Operational data	[16, 18, 23, 24, 26, 28, 34–36, 40–42, 44–46, 49, 51, 52, 54, 55, 59–62, 64, 65]
Data from logs and reports	[25, 27, 36, 51, 64]
Simulation data	[26, 57, 63, 65]
Speed and acceleration data	[11, 12, 14, 34, 37, 43, 45, 50, 52]
Temperature	[21, 22, 25, 37, 46, 49, 50, 62]
Track geometry	[11, 12, 17, 21, 27, 37, 55, 56]
Vibration measurements	[13, 15, 20, 41]
Weather conditions	[24, 27, 37, 49, 62]

refined strategy based on the characteristics of the sleepers used to identify the fastener, introducing Haar-like features pertinent to the geometry of the fastener characteristics.

Inspection of tracks, degradation analysis and early FD are also present in the literature. Authors in [11, 12] implement Machine Learning (ML) models and acceleration data to predict track degradation. The DL model proposed in [13] integrates Convolutional Neural Networks (CNN) and Long Short-Term Memory (LSTM) models for track quality evaluation in High-Speed Railways (HSR) networks. The proposed solution relies on the prediction of vehicle-body vibrations and takes advantage of the powerful feature extraction capacities of CNN and LSTM models. The authors in [14] also use acceleration data measured from sensors in combination with Artificial Neural Networks (ANNs) to identify track defects. While the authors in [15] propose a DL solution for railway track inspection that implements collaborative CNN-based detection models. Authors in [16] propose a solar-powered autonomous vehicle for FD of cracks in the railway line. The robot includes an infrared sensor to detect obstacles, an ultrasonic sensor to detect the distance to track surface and finding abnormalities, a GPS positioning, and a communication module to provide location data. The study presented in [17] combines ML, Support Vector Machines (SVMs), ANNs, random forest and more to assemble a multilayer model for Fault Prognosis (FP) in rails. For the case study, the authors feed the ensemble model with matching track geometry and a defect dataset that includes approximately 50000 rail defects harvested from data spanning 35000 km of track and over five years of inspection. Authors in [18] implement DL for processing data harvested from smart sensors and IoT devices for FD in railway tracks. The authors in [19] proposed a DL-based approach for the conditional monitoring of thermite welded joints in rails using an onboard camera and CNNs. This solution proposes the implementation of an onboard camera or sensor to collect the images necessary for the visual inspection of joints in real-time. Finally, the study [20] describes a model based on LSTM Recurrent Neural Networks for the Fault Detection and Diagnosis (FDD) of railway tracks. The proposed solution is based on commonly available measurement signals from multiple track circuits; faults are diagnosed from their spatial and temporal dependencies.

There are other approaches. The study [21] propose a hybrid fiber optics sensor system, based on Fibre Bragg Grating (FBG) and Raman Distributed Temperature Sensing (RDTS) for real-time monitoring of railway track geometrical data for the detection of longitudinal, horizontal and cross-level defects. The authors in [22] combine thermal images with fuzzy logic for the maintenance of electric railway lines. And [23] implements microcontrollers to detect loosened bolts in railway's fishplates using data collected from an electrical pulse generator device.

The maintenance of railway switches is a recurring topic in the literature. Authors in [24] propose a sample-adaptive Multi-Kernel Learning model for FP in railway points. Domain experts were consulted to aid the authors in building different kernels. The proposed model considers the missing pattern of data and inherent variances in different sets of railway points. The study [25] implements a Data Mining (DM) solution to determine failure causes. The approach is based on text mining and document analysis of large numbers of text verbatims for knowledge extraction. Data related to railway switches include operation times, types, location and weather conditions. The authors in [26] present a model based on Deep Autoencoders and Transfer Learning for unsupervised FD. The proposed model addresses some of the limitations of the available data for FD, and implements clustering algorithms and knowledge from experts, apart from simulated and real data. The authors in [27] present an AI model based on

RegARIMA and LSTM-ANNs to predict the size of the gap in railway switches based on temperature, weather forecast data and history size of the switch gap.

Other parts of the railway circuits are also mentioned in the literature. The study presented in [29] presents a framework based on Computer Vision (CV) and an image acquisition system based on onboard cameras to automate the inspection of railway plugs. And the study presented in [28] describes a Knowledged-based System (KBS) for a FD system for railway track circuits using spatial and temporal data.

Rolling Stock Maintenance. Some of the papers specific to rolling stock maintenance implement AI solutions for the inspection of small parts and other components. For instance, authors in [30] implement CV techniques for identifying small bottom train parts using image data obtained from onboard cameras. The authors in [31] present a FD method for train wagons plug doors based on multi-scale normalized permutation entropy and a multiclass SVM based on Improved Particle Swarm Optimization (PSO) and sound signals data. Another approach by [32] proposes the use of DL for automating the inspection of wagon components. The authors describe an image classification approach based on CNN to detect damages in the wagon's shear pad to avoid train derailments. The model is capable of identifying three states or conditions in shear pads: absent, damaged and undamaged. The study [33] proposes a model that combines cascade learning, ML and CV for inspecting speed sensors in intelligent locomotive vehicles. To solve problems related to poor quality image data (including complex background, motion blur, muddy noise, and variable shapes) the authors present a framework that uses ensemble learning and deals with the problem of imbalanced data. It includes two learning stages: target localization and speed sensor detection. The authors conclude that a similar approach can be implemented in other areas of asset maintenance. Another study [34] proposes an automated DL-based FDD network system for vehicle on-board equipment. The authors formulate the fault diagnosis problem mathematically, including the definition of fault evidence vectors and reason vectors by analyzing operational data collected from HSRs. A Deep Belief Network (DBN) is developed and trained on the basis of a Restricted Boltzmann Machine and validated with real-world data. The study [35], propose a learning model based on ML and supervised pattern recognition for wagon repairing based on the human activity in production and knowledge from experts. The study [22] implements fuzzy logic for the maintenance of the pantograph and catenary systems in electric railways using thermal images.

Several papers are centered on the wheels in the rolling stock vehicles. For instance, the authors in [36] propose a DM approach for FP in wheels using data available from maintenance and operational activities. Whereas the authors in [37] use ANNs to determine the adhesion between wheels and rails. Adhesion between wheels and rails during operation is determined by many factors, making its estimation a complex task. Some other approaches presented by the authors include model-based prediction, inverse dynamic modelling, Kalman filter method, and a PSO method. The input data collected with sensors, and the definition of validation and training datasets are fundamental factors to be considered when choosing the correct model. In [38, 39] the authors propose a model based in CV and a Differential Evolution (DE) algorithm for estimating the size of rollingstock wheels to ensure stability in HSRs. The system proposed is based on the detection of images, and implements a combination of optical intercept image direction and an ANN prediction model based on Levenberg-Marquardt back propagation; this is complemented with a DE algorithm to optimize the initial connection weights and thresholds in the ANN. The authors in [40] present a condition-based monitoring model for train wheels that implements FBG sensors. These sensors can detect imperfections (such as flange pits, wheel flats and polygonal wheels) as they will produce an uneven strain impulse on the track in contrast to a symmetrical strain impulse from a defect-free piece. The authors in [41] propose a model for the diagnosis of faults in wagon wheelsets based on an Adaptative Swarm Optimization DBN algorithm and using the wheels vibration signals as input data. Another study [42], proposes a ML model for on-board wheel classification based on vehicle dynamics. The authors study the physical effects using a multi body dynamics model of a freight wagon in different scenarios and operational conditions.

Rolling stock monitoring is also present in the literature. The study [43] presents a ML model that uses vertical acceleration data to monitor the performance of rolling stock. And the authors in [44] presents a ML model for the predictive maintenance of rolling stock that avoids the interruption of service while providing Reliability, Availability, Maintainability, and Safety (RAMS) standards. This solution implements IoT devices and smart sensors embedded in rolling stock in order to collect data. The propose architecture allows the direct transmission of valuable data such as detected anomalies and the geopositioning of rolling stock. These data are then fed to a ML algorithm for the prediction of the maintenance cycle and the calculation of the remaining useful life of railway assets. Authors in [45] propose a system for monitoring the combustion locomotive based on data collected with IoT devices. GPS signals are used to obtain the geographical location of the vehicle and combined with accelerometers and gyroscopic Micro Electro-Mechanical Systems sensors to infer movement parameters and velocity. Some of the critical situations that can be detected by this device include diesel locomotive engine dysfunctions, high vibrations and the exceeding of limit velocity, acceleration, or inclination. The system also offers registration of vibroacoustic signals for online locomotive diagnosis, the reconstruction of trajectory, path and position of the vehicle, and the detection of damage based on exceeding vibrations. Similarly, authors in [46] propose unsupervised anomaly detection models based on autoencoders and isolation forest algorithms for heavy haul operations using data harvested from IoT devices. There is a vast amount of data available from the use of sensors and their maintenance history: these data can be used to detect, identify and ultimately predict treat faults in heavy haul operations. The data utilized to evaluate these models were harvested from real measurements obtained from thermal, acoustic and impact sensors.

Infrastructure Maintenance. Some of the maintenance-related tasks are focused on railway infrastructure. Different AI-based solutions are proposed. For instance, authors in [21] propose a monitoring system for large railway infrastructures essential sites based on FBGs and RDTS sensors. The proposed model is aim at a real-time monitoring of essential sites in large railway infrastructures (such as bridges, viaducts and slopes that are prone to landslides) as well the geometrical condition of the railway tracks. The study presented in [47] implements the YOLOv3 DL algorithm for the analysis of concrete surface cracks in railway bridges. The data to test the model are acquired implementing four CCD cameras followed by a careful selection of training images. A total of 100 images were classified and enhanced to generate 3000 fracture examples. The authors in [48] present multi-frame image analysis for the management and maintenance of rail-side facilities. The images captured by cameras mounted on the front end of trains are used to elicit information on the railway environment. Unlike current image segmentation analysis, the proposed model implements a multi-frame analysis that considers temporal continuity based on optical flow calculations between sequential frames and pixel-wise processing. The model was trained using existing datasets as well as images captured by the researchers and tested in different scenarios and configurations. The authors in [49] implement fuzzy-knowledge-based ANNs for ticket machine maintenance in high transit railway stations. Experts in the field are consulted and their input is transformed into membership functions used to train this model. Other inputs include operational, weather and temperature data.

Another task presented in the literature is the maintenance of the catenary system and neutral sections. In [50] the authors use a ML approach for FD and remote monitoring of neutral sections in railway networks. This model implements ML techniques to accurately assess and classify failures and abnormalities. Data on the neutral sections is harvested using accelerometers and non-contact infrared thermometer sensors to monitor the interaction between the pantograph and contact wire. The authors in [51] introduce an unsupervised anomaly detection system based on autoencoders for the condition monitoring of railway catenary systems. The trained autoencoders can identify anomalous data indicating possible defects on the catenary; these data are then contrasted with real historical data. The authors in [52] present a data-driven condition-monitoring model based on Bayesian Networks (BN). The model contains nodes based on the physical relationships of the data types collected during inspection, including train speed, dynamic stagger and height of the contact wire, pantograph head acceleration, and pantograph-catenary contact force. The probability tables of the BN are estimated using historical inspection data and maintenance records. Finally, authors in [53] present a CV approach for FD in catenary systems based on image data. The proposed model counts with three different stages and relies on image processing techniques and DL methodologies that consider the configuration of the catenary system.

The maintenance of geological infrastructure also appears in the literature. The study in [54] presents automized ML and DL models that identify soil erosion in railway infrastructures using remote sensors. The model proposed is fed with data from these sensors, and also includes a training dataset of 2000 high-resolution images. The authors in [55] propose a SVM model optimized with a genetic algorithm to prevent train derailments. This solution differs from their previous studies [11, 12] on the datasets implemented, which are not based on acceleration data, but in different parameters including track gauge deviation, traffic data and structural parameters. Finally, the study presented in [56] proposes using track geometry data extracted from sensors for detecting instability in railway embankments.

Monitoring. The literature shows that AI solutions can also be implemented for the general monitoring and assessment of railway systems. Different approaches are suggested. The study [51] presents a condition monitoring system for railway catenary systems based on anomaly detection using autoencoders. Autoencoders are used to reduce the dimensionality of multisensor data and generate discriminative features to distinguish healthy and anomalous data. The authors evaluate the model with real historical data from HSRs. Authors in [57] present a framework for condition-based maintenance in dynamic environments based on agent theory and simulation data. They present an organizational design framework that provides a representation of requirements and control mechanisms to switch between different contextual states as a response to external changes in dynamic environments. The purpose of the framework is to specify a mechanism to coordinate the behaviour of operational agents in collaboration to achieve a common objective. In [50] the authors use a ML approach for the remote monitoring of neutral sections in railway networks. Data on the interaction between the pantograph and contact wire is collected using accelerometers and thermometer sensors. ML is used to classify failures and abnormalities. The authors in [52] present a data-driven condition-monitoring model for railway catenaries based on BNs. The BN's nodes are based on operational data. Inspection data and maintenance records are used to estimate the network's probability tables. The authors in [58] present a domain-specific modelling language that can be used to generate models such as BNs and Petri Nets to evaluate the RAMS standards in railways. The data utilized is based on the proposed modelling language, that extends the UML model to railway-related applications. This allows domain experts and railway modelers to design solutions at a conceptual representation level, using familiar expressions and methodologies related to the field.

The implementation of different IoT devices is a recurring approach in the literature. For instance, the authors in [59] discuss different sensor configurations and topologies for the application of Wireless Sensor Networks (WSNs) for conditional monitoring of railways. This study is a comparative review of practical engineering solutions where sensor devices are used for the monitoring and analysis of systems, structures, vehicles, and machinery. Different sensor configurations and network topologies are identified and discussed, including communication medium utilized, transmission and routing of data and fixed and movable types of monitoring devices. This condition monitoring systems must store large quantities of data; that can later be processed and combined with different algorithms to identify faults in real-time. Some considerations are the treatment of noisy data and data loss, as well as the implementation of contextual data to improve the model's coverage and accuracy. The authors in [60] propose a universal platform for real-time condition-based asset monitoring and surveillance utilizing data collected with IoT devices. They propose a centralized model for the real-time assessment of assets such as the track, overhead lines, rolling stock, point machines and more as a Decision Support System (DSS) to ensure the train service RAMS standards. The study presented in [61] proposes the implementation of WSNs for the monitoring of railway bridges for maintenance purposes. The model functions by triggering data recollection once the train is approaching the bridge, the data are sent to an onboard sink node for its analysis based on different operational scenarios. The authors in [21] propose a holistic real-time monitoring system for large railway infrastructures (including essential infrastructure and railway tracks) based on the analysis of railway track geometrical data using FBGs and RDTS sensors. Whereas authors in [62] implement a fuzzy rule-based model to recognize the abnormal state of railway infrastructure. The different fuzzy rules were created with data collected from IoT devices. The input data includes railroad temperature, intrusion detectors, number of passengers and railroad snowdrift detectors.

Maintenance Planning. The planning of maintenance activities is also an important topic in the literature. The authors in [63] present a study on the applicability of ML and simulations in the development of DSSs for tactical and operational planning of track circuits maintenance. The framework implements one-class SVM to build the data driven model, BNs for modelling and simulation and MILP mathematical models for optimization. Two different case studies are presented: one for strategic earthworks asset management, and the other for tactical and operational planning of track circuits maintenance. The applicability of the framework proves to be a generic and adaptable tool for DSS in railway asset management and performance monitoring. The authors in [64] implement fuzzy comprehension evaluation for maintainability allocation. To determine an index of maintainability, some parameter options are considered such as mean time to repair, mean active preventive, mean active corrective and maximum corrective maintenance time, as well as maintenance downtime. Other data includes user requirements, maintainability levels of similar products, life cycle cost, and more. The study [65] presents a choice function hyper-heuristic framework for the allocation of maintenance tasks in railway networks. The authors model the problem as a Multi-Depot Vehicle Routing Problem (MDVRP) using routes and geographical location data, the model implements perturbative hyper-heuristics for the assignment of maintenance tasks to crew members. A search is performed on a single starting candidate solution that is improved on every iteration of the algorithm.

4 Discussion

A Shift from Symbolic AI to ML-Based AI. An observable pattern throughout this study is the shift from symbolic AI to ML and heuristic-based solutions in the last decades. Numerical-based AI models are powerful and effective. Nonetheless, there is a negative side to this, the explainability, comprehension and interpretability of AI become more obscure as complexity increases, affecting the general trustworthiness of a model. This is important in railway applications such as maintenance, where errors can be translated into fatalities. Hence there is hesitation on the utilization of black-box AI models. These models lack explainability and transparency in contrast to traditional AI approaches which may be intrinsically comprehensible. Models must be evaluated thoroughly before they can be deployed. This can be overcome with exhausting testing and various techniques to make these models more transparent and easier to understand.

Symbolic AI applications are recurrent in the literature both as standalone solutions and in combination with numerical-based AI models. Some symbolic AI methods recurring in the literature related to railway maintenance include KBS [28, 35, 49], fuzzy logic [22, 62, 64] and computer simulations [26, 57, 63, 65]. Moreover, hybrid combinations of traditional methods with numerical-based AI models are observed in the literature [28, 35, 39, 44, 49]. For instance, the knowledge of experts can be utilized and replicated in computer systems creating KBS that also consider outputs from black-box AI models such as ANN or BN [28, 35, 49].

Computer Vision. The advance of Machine Learning, Artificial Neural Networks and other numerical models has contributed greatly to modern applications in the maintenance of the railway sector. For instance, Deep Neural Networks implemented for CV can aid the detection and tracking of objects in real-time [19, 30]. CV techniques also allow for images reconstruction and classification and can be implemented for different areas of the railway sector. The continuous monitoring of assets and the automation of maintenance activities can also ensure the safety of passengers and railway workers. For instance, obstacle detection and monitoring of the state of the railway tracks [19, 29, 54]. Many papers consulted in the literature used computer vision for asset monitoring and abnormality detection [9, 10, 19, 32, 33, 38, 39, 53], identification of assets [30, 39], and situation analysis [19] among other applications.

IoT Devices and Smart Sensors. An observable pattern in the literature is the complementation of IoT devices and smart sensors with Data Mining approaches [16, 18, 23, 24, 26, 28, 34–36, 40–42, 44–46, 49, 51, 52, 54, 55, 59–62, 64, 65]. Data harvested with this methodology are usually later used to feed a ML or ANN models. These real-time data can be utilized to feed powerful numeric-based AI models for railway-maintenance-related tasks.

The implementation of WSN for different applications in the sector such as infrastructure monitoring and surveillance are found in the literature [59, 61]. These devices are easy to install and setup, and can be acquired for a low cost, this makes WSNs easy to maintenance and power. WSNs can be complemented with smart sensors that are capable of reading and understanding the railway environment. More powerful models based on ML and ANNs can be implemented to recognize patterns and aid with the identification of complex events. The response to any complex events identified can be either automated or used as a DSS to aid experts and railway operators.

Data Used for Railway Maintenance AI Models. While the most common type of data mentioned in the literature correspond to numerical and text data; data from other railway-maintenance-related operations can be obtained from different sources, including video and image data [9, 10, 19, 22, 29, 30, 32–34, 38, 39, 47, 48, 53, 54], operational data elicited from different sensors and IoT devices [16, 18, 23, 24, 26, 28, 34–36, 40–42, 44–46, 49, 51, 52, 54, 55, 59–62, 64, 65], train speed and acceleration measurements [11, 12, 14, 34, 37, 43, 45, 50, 52], acoustic and sound data [16, 31, 45, 46], vibration measurements [13, 15, 20, 41], GPS coordinates and location data [16, 28, 34, 44, 45, 65], track geometry data [11, 12, 17, 21, 27, 37, 55, 56], temperature data [21, 22, 25, 37, 46, 49, 50, 62], knowledge from experts [24, 26, 35, 49, 58] and more. As we have observed in our previous research, other sources of data can also contribute to a model creation [1, 8]. Examples includes data on weather conditions [24, 27, 37, 49, 62], historical data from logs and reports [25, 27, 36, 51, 64] and data generated from heuristic approaches and computer simulations [26, 57, 63, 65].

Powerful ML models, such as ANN and DM techniques, can use the power of IoT devices and smart sensors for the collection of real-time data on a functioning train to make different predictions. For instance, one type of data that emerge in various papers is acceleration data. Acceleration data has many applications in maintenance such as real-time rolling stock monitoring and the prediction or identification of possible failures of train parts and railway assets. Many authors have generated their own datasets by implementing mounted cameras and other smart sensors in order to capture data in real time. This process can be exhausting and time consuming. Fortunately, the flexibility and versatility of IoT devices is making this task much easier. Transfer learning can also be a good solution for this problem, but some cases are delicate enough that special datasets must be created for their proper functioning. The same is the case for data harvested from computer simulations.

In our previous research, we have found a great number of supporting railway datasets and APIs that are openly available to the public. These data can be implemented in AI models for complementary purposes. Furthermore, real-time data can be harvested from these publicly available sources to create new datasets that can later be used to feed AI models [1, 8].

5 Conclusion

Our literature review reveals that the possible applications of AI in the railway sector are vast. There are many tasks related to railway maintenance that can greatly benefit from AI applications. We have analyzed the state of the art by summarizing different tasks and problems belonging to the maintenance of railway operations and common AI-based models implemented for their solution.

Our research shows a rapid increase on the number of research papers on the topic. This growth is somewhat accompanied – to a lesser extent – with that of publicly available AI-oriented datasets [8]. Despite this, there is still a huge gap between available research papers and public datasets. Another observable pattern throughout this study is the shift from symbolic AI to ML and heuristic-based solutions in the last years, along with the implementation of IoT devices and smart sensors for railway maintenance operations. Great results might be obtained from these models, but their intrinsic complexity and lack of traceability render the systems unreliable for some applications. This factor is an important part of the application of AI in some sensitive areas of the railway sector such as the one discussed in this paper.

The railway sector is broad and complex; data from railway operations can be obtained from different sources, including video and image data, train speed and acceleration measurements, sound recordings and acoustic data, vibration measurements, GPS coordinates, track geometry data, temperature data, knowledge from experts and more. Powerful ML models, such as ANN, and DM techniques can use the power of IoT devices and smart sensors for the collection of real-time data on a functioning train to make different predictions. We have also observed that other sources of data can also contribute to the creation of AI models; examples include data on weather conditions, historical logs and operational data, statistical data, and technical reports among others.

This work has been partially supported by Uppsala University and the project KAJT - Capacity in the Railway Traffic System (Kapacitet i Järnvägstrafiken), a Swedish research program for improved railway system performance. This was possible under the grant agreement numbers TRV/2020/119576 and TRV/2021/59020. The author declares no conflict of interest.

References

1. Pappaterra, M.J.: A literature and public datasets review for the application of AI in the railway industry. Dissertation, Uppsala Universitet, Uppsala, Sweden (2022)
2. Tang, R., et al.: A literature review of Artificial Intelligence applications in railway systems. Transp. Res. Part C Emerg. Technol. **140**, 103679 (2022)
3. Chenariyan Nakhaee, M., Hiemstra, D., Stoelinga, M., van Noort, M.: The recent applications of machine learning in rail track maintenance: a survey. In: Collart-Dutilleul, S., Lecomte, T., Romanovsky, A. (eds.) Reliability, Safety, and Security of Railway Systems. Modelling, Analysis, Verification, and Certification. LNCS, pp. 91–105. Springer, Cham (2019). https://doi.org/10.1007/978-3-030-18744-6_6
4. Thilagavathy, N., Harene, J., Sherine, M., Shanmugasundari, T.: Survey on railway wheel defect detection using machine learning. AutAut Res. J. **11**(4), 4 (2020)
5. Hamadache, M., Dutta, S., Olaby, O., Ambur, R., Stewart, E., Dixon, R.: On the fault detection and diagnosis of railway switch and crossing systems: an overview. Appl. Sci. Open Access J. **9**(5129), 1–32 (2019)
6. Liu, S., Wang, Q., Luo, Y.: A review of applications of visual inspection technology based on image processing in the railway industry. Transp. Saf. Environ. **1**(3), 185–204 (2019)
7. De Donato, L., et al.: A survey on audio-video based defect detection through deep learning in railway maintenance. IEEE Access (2022)
8. Pappaterra, M.J., Flammini, F., Vittorini, V., Bešinović, N.: A systematic review of artificial intelligence public datasets for railway applications. Infrastructures **6**(10), 136 (2021). https://doi.org/10.3390/infrastructures6100136
9. Wei, X., Yang, Z., Liu, Y., Wei, D., Jia, L., Li, Y.: Railway track fastener defect detection based on image processing and deep learning techniques: a comparative study. Eng. Appl. Artif. Intell. **80**, 66–81 (2019)
10. Xia, Y., Xie, F., Jiang, Z.: Broken railway fastener detection based on AdaBoost algorithm. In: 2010 International Conference on Optoelectronics and Image Processing, vol. 1, pp. 313–316 (2010)
11. Falamarzi, A., Moridpour, S., Nazem, M., Cheraghi, S.: Development of random forests regression model to predict track degradation index: Melbourne case study. In: Australian Transport Research Forum (2018)
12. Falamarzi, A., Moridpour, S., Nazem, M.: Development of a tram track degradation prediction model based on the acceleration data. Struct. Infrastruct. Eng. **15**(10), 1308–1318 (2019)
13. Ma, S., Gao, L., Liu, X., Lin, J.: Deep learning for track quality evaluation of high-speed railway based on vehicle-body vibration prediction. IEEE Access **7**, 185099–185107 (2019). https://doi.org/10.1109/ACCESS.2019.2960537
14. Bahamon-Blanco, S., Rapp, S., Rupp, C., Liu, J., Martin, U.: Recognition of track defects through measured acceleration - part 1. In: IOP Conference Series: Materials Science and Engineering, vol. 615, pp. 1–8 (2019)
15. Gibert, X., Patel, V.M., Chellappa, R.: Deep multitask learning for railway track inspection. IEEE Trans. Intell. Transp. Syst. **18**(1), 153–164 (2016)
16. Salvi, S., Shetty, S.: AI based solar powered railway track crack detection and notification system with chatbot support. In: 2019 Third International Conference on I-SMAC (IoT in Social, Mobile, Analytics and Cloud) (I-SMAC), pp. 565–571 (2019)

17. Lasisi, A., Attoh-Okine, N.: Machine learning ensembles and rail defects prediction: multi-layer stacking methodology. ASCE-ASME J. Risk Uncertain. Eng. Syst. A: Civ. Eng. **5**(4), 04019016 (2019)
18. Niebling, J., Baasch, B., Kruspe, A.: Analysis of railway track irregularities with convolutional autoencoders and clustering algorithms. In: Bernardi, S., et al. (eds.) EDCC 2020. CCIS, vol. 1279, pp. 78–89. Springer, Cham (2020). https://doi.org/10.1007/978-3-030-58462-7_7
19. Liu, Y., Sun, X., Pang, J. H. L.: A YOLOv3-based deep learning application research for condition monitoring of rail thermite welded joints. In: Proceedings of the 2020 2nd International Conference on Image, Video and Signal Processing (IVSP 2020), NY, Association for Computing Machinery, pp. 33–38 (2020). https://doi.org/10.1145/3388818.3388827. Accessed 20 Aug 2021
20. de Bruin, T., Verbert, K., Babuška, R.: Railway track circuit fault diagnosis using recurrent neural networks. IEEE Trans. Neural Netw. Learn. Syst. **28**(3), 523–533 (2016)
21. Velha, P., et al: Monitoring large railways infrastructures using hybrid FBG/Raman sensor systems. In: 20th Italian National Conference on Photonic Technologies (Fotonica 2018), pp. 1–3 (2018) https://doi.org/10.1049/cp.2018.1644
22. Karakose, M., Yaman, O.: Complex fuzzy system based predictive maintenance approach in railways. IEEE Trans. Industr. Inform. **16**(9), 6023–6032 (2020). https://doi.org/10.1109/TII.2020.2973231
23. Nayan, M.M.R., Al Sufi, S., Abedin, A.K., Ahamed, R., Hossain, M. F.: An IoT based real-time railway fishplate monitoring system for early warning. In: 2020 11th International Conference on Electrical and Computer Engineering (ICECE), pp. 310–313 (2020). https://doi.org/10.1109/ICECE51571.2020.9393036
24. Li, Z., Zhang, J., Wu, Q., Gong, Y., Yi, J., Kirsch, C.: Sample adaptive multiple kernel learning for failure prediction of railway points. In: Proceedings of the 25th ACM SIGKDD International Conference on Knowledge Discovery & Data Mining, pp. 2848–2856 (2019)
25. Lin, C., Wang, G.: Failure cause extraction of railway switches based on text mining. In: Proceedings of the 2017 International Conference on Computer Science and Artificial Intelligence, ser. CSAI 2017. NY, Association for Computing Machinery, pp. 237–241 (2017). https://doi.org/10.1145/3168390.3168402. Accessed 26 July 2020
26. Guo, Z., Wan, Y., Ye, H.: An unsupervised fault-detection method for railway turnouts. IEEE Trans. Instrum. Meas. **69**(11), 8881–8901 (2020). https://doi.org/10.1109/TIM.2020.2998863
27. Li, C., Zhao, L., Cai, B.: Size prediction of railway switch gap based on RegARIMA model and LSTM network. IEEE Access **8**, 198188–198200 (2020). https://doi.org/10.1109/ACCESS.2020.3034687
28. Verbert, K., De Schutter, B., Babuška, R.: Fault diagnosis using spatial and temporal information with application to railway track circuits. Eng. Appl. Artif. Intell. **56**, 200–211 (2016)
29. Du, X., Cheng, Y., Gu, Z.: Change detection: the framework of visual inspection system for railway plug defects. IEEE Access **8**, 152161–152172 (2020). https://doi.org/10.1109/ACCESS.2020.3017691
30. Xin, Z., Lu, T., Li, X.: Detection of train bottom parts based on XIoU. In: RSVT 2019: Proceedings of the 2019 International Conference on Robotics Systems and Vehicle Technology, pp. 91–96 (2019). https://doi.org/10.1145/3366715.3366742. Accessed 26 July 2020
31. Sun, Y., Xie, G., Cao, Y., Wen, T.: A fault diagnosis method for train plug doors based on MNPE and IPSO-MSVM. In: 2018 International Conference on Control, Automation and Information Sciences (ICCAIS), pp. 467–471 (2018)
32. Rocha, R.L., et al.: A deep-learning-based approach for automated wagon component inspection, pp. 276–283 (2018)

33. Li, B., et al.: A cascade learning approach for automated detection of locomotive speed sensor using imbalanced data in ITS. IEEE Access **7**(18843598), 90851–90862 (2019). https://doi.org/10.1109/ACCESS.2019.2928224
34. Yin, J., Zhao, W.: Fault diagnosis network design for vehicle onboard equipments of high-speed railway: a deep learning approach. Eng. Appl. Artif. Intell. **56**, 250–259 (2016)
35. Tsyganov, V.: Decision making and learning in wagon-repairing. In: 2019 Twelfth International Conference Management of Large-Scale System Development (MLSD), Moscow, Russia, pp. 1–5 (2019)
36. Yang, C., Létourneau, S.: Learning to predict train wheel failures. In: KDD 2005: Proceedings of the Eleventh ACM SIGKDD International Conference on Knowledge Discovery in Data Mining, pp. 516–525 (2005). https://doi.org/10.1145/1081870.1081929. Accessed 26 July 2020
37. Shrestha, S., Wu, Q., Spiryagin, M.: Review of adhesion estimation approaches for rail vehicles. Int. J. Rail Transp. **7**(2), 79–102 (2019)
38. Zhang, J., Zhang, Y., Luo, L., Gao, X., Ling, Z.: Neural network optimization and high-speed railway wheel-set size prediction forecasting based on differential evolution. In: Wang, H. (ed.) Eleventh International Conference on Information Optics and Photonics (CIOP 2019), vol. 11209, pp. 1301–1309. International Society for Optics and Photonics. SPIE (2019). https://doi.org/10.1117/12.2550065. Accessed 26 July 2020
39. Zhang, Y., Zhang, J., Luo, L., Gao, X.: Optimization of LMPB high-speed railway wheel size prediction algorithm based on improved adaptive differential evolution algorithm. Int. J. Distrib. Sens. Netw. **15**(10), 1550147719881348 (2019). https://doi.org/10.1177/155014771 9881348. Accessed 26 July 2020
40. Ho, S.L., et al.: A comprehensive condition monitoring of modern railway. In: 2006 IET International Conference on Railway Condition Monitoring, pp. 125–129 (2006)
41. Wang, H., Li, H., Li, Y., Duan, Y.: Railway wagon wheelset fault diagnosis method based on DBN. In: 2020 Global Reliability and Prognostics and Health Management (PHM-Shanghai), pp. 1–6 (2020). https://doi.org/10.1109/PHM-Shanghai49105.2020.9280980
42. Luber, B., Sorribes-Palmer, F., Müller, G., Pietsch, L., Six, K.: On-board wheel profile classification based on vehicle dynamics - from physical effects to machine learning. In: Klomp, M., Bruzelius, F., Nielsen, J., Hillemyr, A. (eds.) IAVSD 2019. LNME, pp. 113–118. Springer, Cham (2020). https://doi.org/10.1007/978-3-030-38077-9_13
43. Shafiullah, G.M., Simson, S., Thompson, A., Wolfs, P.J., Shawkat, A.A.: Monitoring vertical acceleration of railway wagon using machine learning technique, pp. 770–775 (2008)
44. Nappi, R., Striano, V., Cutrera, G., Vigliotti, A., Franzè, G.: Rolling stocks: a machine learning predictive maintenance architecture. In: Bernardi, S., et al. (eds.) EDCC 2020. CCIS, vol. 1279, pp. 68–77. Springer, Cham (2020). https://doi.org/10.1007/978-3-030-58462-7_6
45. Boguś, P., Merkisz, J., Grzeszczyk, R.: Monitoring of combustion locomotive state with the use of an on-board device. In: COMPRAIL 2014, vol. 135, pp. 319–326 (2014). https://doi.org/10.2495/CR140261
46. Oliveira, D.F., et al.: Evaluating unsupervised anomaly detection models to detect faults in heavy haul railway operations. In: 2019 18th IEEE International Conference on Machine Learning and Applications (ICMLA), pp. 1016–1022 (2019)
47. XingQi, G., Quan, L., MeiLing, Z., HuiFeng, J.: Analysis and test of concrete surface crack of railway bridge based on deep learning. In: 2020 IEEE 5th Information Technology and Mechatronics Engineering Conference (ITOEC), pp. 437–442 (2020). https://doi.org/10.1109/ITOEC49072.2020.9141789
48. Furitsu, Y., et al.: Semantic segmentation of railway images considering temporal continuity. In: Palaiahnakote, S., Sanniti di Baja, G., Wang, L., Yan, W.Q. (eds.) ACPR 2019. LNCS, vol. 12046, pp. 639–652. Springer, Cham (2020). https://doi.org/10.1007/978-3-030-41404-7_45

49. Liu, J.N., Sin, K.Y.: Fuzzy neural networks for machine maintenance in mass transit railway system. IEEE Trans. Neural Netw. **8**(4), 932–941 (1997)
50. Phala, K., Doorsamy, W., Paul, B.S.: Detection and clustering of neutral section faults using machine learning techniques for SMART railways. In: 2019 6th International Conference on Soft Computing Machine Intelligence (ISCMI), pp. 1–6 (2019)
51. Wang, H.: Unsupervised anomaly detection in railway catenary condition monitoring using autoencoders. In: IECON 2020 The 46th Annual Conference of the IEEE Industrial Electronics Society, pp. 2636–2641 (2020). https://doi.org/10.1109/IECON43393.2020.925 4633
52. Wang, H., Nunez, A., Liu, Z., Zhang, D., Dollevoet, R.: A Bayesian network approach for condition monitoring of high-speed railway catenaries. IEEE Trans. Intell. Transp. Syst. **21**(10), 4037–4051 (2020). https://doi.org/10.1109/TITS.2019.2934346
53. Huang, C., Zeng, Y.: The fault diagnosis of catenary system based on the deep learning method in the railway industry, pp. 135–140 (2020)
54. Nogueira, K., LS Machado, G., HT Gama, P., CV da Silva, C., Balaniuk, R., A. dos Santos, J.: Facing erosion identification in railway lines using pixel-wise deep-based approaches. Remote Sens. **12**(4), 739 (2020)
55. Falamarzi, A., Moridpour, S., Nazem, M., Hesami, R.: Integration of genetic algorithm and support vector machine to predict rail track degradation. In: MATEC Web of Conferences, vol. 259, pp. 1–5, no. 02007 (2019)
56. Kite, D., Siino, G., Audley, M.: Detecting embankment instability using measurable track geometry data. Infrastructures **5**(3), 29 (2020)
57. Jiang, J., Huisman, B., Dignum, V.: Agent-based multiorganizational interaction design: a case study of the Dutch railway system. vol. 2, pp. 196–203 (2012)
58. Bernardi, S., et al.: Enabling the usage of UML in the verification of railway systems: the dam-rail approach. Reliab. Eng. Syst. Saf. **120**, 112–126 (2013)
59. Hodge, V.J., O'Keefe, S., Weeks, M., Moulds, A.: Wireless sensor networks for condition monitoring in the railway industry: a survey. IEEE Trans. Intell. Transp. Syst. **16**(3), 1088–1106 (2014)
60. Lee, T., Tso, M.: A universal sensor data platform modelled for real-time asset condition surveillance and big data analytics for railway systems: developing a railway mastermind for the betterment of reliability, availability, maintainability and safety of railway systems and passenger service. In: 2016 IEEE Sensors, pp. 1–3 (2016)
61. Chebrolu, K., Raman, B., Mishra, N., Valiveti, P.K., Kumar, R.: Brimon: a sensor network system for railway bridge monitoring. In: MobiSys 2008 - Proceedings of the 6th International Conference on Mobile Systems, Applications, and Services, 2–14 January 2008, pp. 2–14 (2008). https://doi.org/10.1145/1378600.1378603
62. Jang, G.J., Ahn, T.K., Kim, M.H., Kim, Y.N., Jung, J.Y.: A classifier model for recognition of railway infrastructure abnormal state. In: Proceedings of the 2018 International Conference on Computational Intelligence and Intelligent Systems, ser. CIIS 2018. NY. Association for Computing Machinery, pp. 85–88 (2018). https://doi.org/10.1145/3293475.3293491. Accessed 26 July 2020
63. Consilvio, A., Solís-Hernández, J., Jiménez-Redondo, N., Sanetti, P., Papa, F., Mingolarra-Garaizar, I.: On applying machine learning and simulative approaches to railway asset management, the earthworks and track circuits case studies. Sustainability **12**(6), 2544 (2020)
64. Catelani, M., Ciani, L., Guidi, G., Patrizi, G.: Maintainability improvement using allocation methods for railway systems. Acta IMEKO **9**(1), 10–17 (2020)
65. Pour, S.M., Drake, J.H., Burke, E.K.: A choice function hyper-heuristic framework for the allocation of maintenance tasks in Danish railways. Comput. Oper. Res. **93**, 15–26 (2018). http://www.sciencedirect.com/science/article/pii/S0305054817302423. Accessed 26 July 2020

Synthetic Data Generation for Condition Monitoring of Railway Switches

Miguel del Álamo[1]([✉]), Judith Heusel[1], and Daniela Narezo Guzmán[2][iD]

[1] German Aerospace Center (DLR), Lilienthalplatz 7, 38108 Braunschweig, Germany
[2] German Aerospace Center (DLR), Rutherfordstr. 2, 12489 Berlin, Germany
{miguel.delalamoruiz,judith.heusel,daniela.narezoguzman}@dlr.de

Abstract. The application of AI methods to industry requires a large amount of training data that covers all situations appearing in practice. It is often a challenge to collect a sufficient amount of such data. An alternative is to artificially generate realistic data based on training examples. In this paper we present a method for generating the electric current time series produced by railway switch engines during switchblades repositioning. In practice, this electrical signal is monitored and can be used to detect unusual behaviour associated to switch faults. The generation method requires a sample of real curves and exploits their systematic temperature dependence to reduce their dimensionality. This is done by extracting the effect of temperature on specific parameters, which are then re-sampled and used to generate new curves. The model is analyzed in different practice-relevant scenarios and shows potential for improving condition monitoring methods.

Keywords: Railway switches · Data generation · Anomaly detection

1 Introduction

1.1 Motivation: Anomaly Detection for Railway Switches

Railway switches are an essential element of the railway infrastructure: they are the crossing nodes which allow trains to change tracks. Their condition is safety relevant, since switch faults can lead to accidents and derailments. In addition, switch malfunctions have a negative impact on the infrastructure availability and reputation. Finally, switches are subject to regular maintenance, renewal and repairs, which makes them cost-intensive assets. All of this makes condition-based and predictive maintenance a desirable goal. In order to achieve

---

This project has received funding from the Shift2Rail Joint Undertaking (JU) under grant agreement No 881574. The JU receives support from the European Union's Horizon 2020 research and innovation programme and the Shift2Rail JU members other than the Union. The authors thank Strukton Rail and Wolfgang Riedler for their support on this work.

S. Marrone et al. (Eds.): EDCC 2022 Workshops, CCIS 1656, pp. 76–88, 2022.
https://doi.org/10.1007/978-3-031-16245-9_6

it, continuous monitoring and automatic assessment of the switch condition is required.

Strukton Rail (SR), a Dutch railway infrastructure maintenance operator, monitors the condition of thousands of switches in the Netherlands using the in-house developed system POSS[®][1]. Every time the switch blades are repositioned, POSS[®] collects the electric current at the point machine together with the air temperature at the relay house to which the switch is connected. The electric current at the point machine is a measure of the power needed by the engine to move the switch blades from their start to end position. We refer to the current measured during a single repositioning as current curve. The majority of known switch defects has an influence on the shape of these current curves [1,2].

Within the Shift2Rail project In2Smart2, the German Aerospace Center and SR are developing and validating methods for anomaly detection and diagnosis of switch defects [3]. The goal of these efforts is to support maintenance engineers at SR's Control Center in identifying faulty switches. The project comprises electromechanical switches of type NSE (Nederlandsche Spoorwegen Elektrisch). Current curves of these switches have typically a similar, yet switch- and repositioning direction dependent shape. However, they all are characterised by a systematic temperature dependence (see Fig. 1, [4]). In addition, the curves can be split into segments which roughly correspond to the phases of the blades repositioning (inrush current, unlocking, blades movement and locking, see Fig. 1).

Anomaly detection (AD) approaches applied to current curves can help to identify switch degradation at an early stage as well as sudden failures. Some AD methods (e.g. [4]) employ parameters derived from current curves and their segments (throughout the paper we use the word "parameter" to denote current curve quantities such as length, mean, standard deviation, maximum, kurtosis, etc.). Such models are trained with parameters derived from a set of historical curves for which the switch is assumed to behave normally. The set of historical curves is required to represent typical temperatures found in all seasons.

The validation of AD models is challenging due to the lack of annotated data. The amount of labelled current curves is very low and does not cover a large enough period of time. In this context, the generation of synthetic current curves can help to validate and compare AD models, and to test and improve AD algorithms as well as the considered curve parameters. In addition, it can help to make the current implementation of the AD model more robust by generating realistic data for sparse temperature bins and applicable even when there is few historical data to train the model. This is the case e.g. briefly after a new switch is installed or after maintenance actions are performed on switches, which can strongly modify the current curve typical shape, making it necessary to retrain the AD model. This paper focuses on the generation of synthetic current curves which imitate the normal behaviour of a switch, especially by capturing the temperature dependent variation of the current curves.

---

[1] POSS[®]: Preventief Onderhoud - en Storingsdiagnosesysteem Strukton, http://www. POSSinfo.com.

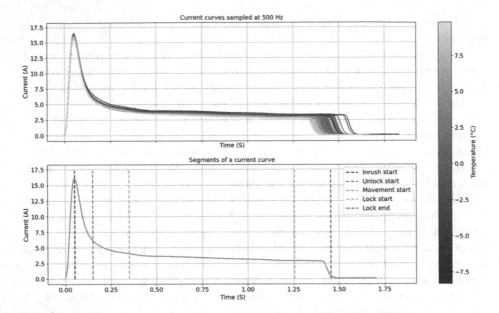

Fig. 1. Upper row: temperature dependence of switch current curves (sampled at 500 Hz). Bottom row: segments of a current curve. The inrush, unlock and lock segments have pre-defined lengths. The curve start is defined as the global maximum's position.

1.2   Challenge: Sampling from a Complex High-Dimensional Distribution

The task of generating new current curves based on real ones can be reformulated as sampling from a high-dimensional distribution. This is a well-known and extremely difficult problem in modern data science (see e.g. [5]).

In our application, temperature is found to be responsible for the main variation in current curves, see Fig. 1. Thus temperature can be used for dimension-reduction. Further, the effect of temperature on the current curves is well captured by three parameters: the curve length, its maximal height, and its median height in the movement segment. In other words, if we take any two curves at different temperatures and manipulate them such that these three parameters match, then they look approximately equal. Two caveats are due here: first, switch condition may change or degrade over time, so this holds for curves measured not too far apart from each other; second, we have tested this phenomenon by taking into account curves from four switches of type NSE. Since switches can vary a lot from one type to another, we do not claim that these three parameters plus temperature are enough to characterize all switch types.

With these observations, the task of sampling from the distribution of curves can be reduced to sampling from their temperature distribution, and then for each temperature, sampling from their parameter distributions, which are all one-dimensional distributions. Finally, the sampled parameters are imposed into an "ideal curve", see Sect. 2. Altogether, this method allows to sample from a complex high-dimensional distribution. Since it is quite flexible, the method can potentially be used in other applications involving electromechanical components.

2   Generation Method and Hyperparameters

2.1   Method Description

Our current curve generation method is based on the sampling methodology discussed in Sect. 1.2, and thus on the effect of temperature on specific parameters (i.e., maximum, length, and median of the movement segment). The underlying assumption is that if the switch is in perfect condition, the shape of the curve does not change and only the three aforementioned parameters vary in dependence on the temperature. In practice, sampling and resolution have an additional impact on the resulting current curves. Due to these assumptions, the curve manipulation for generating new current curves of a given switch is as follows (see Fig. 2 for a schematic workflow visualization): an input curve, which is assumed to be ideal and to represent the current condition of the switch, is chosen per repositioning direction - e.g., the respective first curve of the time series - and serves as model pattern for the synthetically generated ones. Then, the three named parameters are randomly sampled from a temperature-dependent distribution which is learned from real data; details are given in Sect. 2.2. Subsequently the model curve is stretched to have the target length. The resulting curve is then multiplied by a spatially varying scaling function that sets the maximum and the median of the movement segment to the target values.

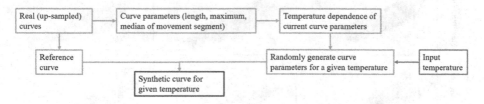

Fig. 2. Description of the process of generating synthetic current curves.

POSS® usually samples current curves at 50 Hz. This sampling rate has a non-negligible effect on the current curves, as it induces discretization issues that add undesired variation and may ruin the generated curves. A way to mitigate this problem is to work with current curves sampled at a higher rate (we employ 500 Hz), which are available only for a few switches. Alternatively the data are up-sampled from 50 to 500 Hz using a section-wise quadratic and linear interpolation, see [3] for details.

2.2 Hyperparameters

In this section we discuss several hyperparameters and variants of our method. As shown in Sect. 3, these variants can have a significant effect on the performance of the simulation results in terms of e.g. distribution similarity of real and synthetic current curve parameters. Moreover, certain variants are specially suitable for particular applications.

Linear vs Empirical Sampling. One key ingredient of the method is the way in which we sample new parameters for a certain temperature given real data. We present two variants here:

1) Empirical method: the new parameter is generated by randomly drawing from the distribution of real parameters in a temperature bin containing the target temperature.
2) Linear method: first we perform a linear regression of the real parameters against temperature. Then the new parameter is randomly sampled from a normal distribution whose mean is given by the linear prediction at that temperature, and whose variance is estimated from real data.

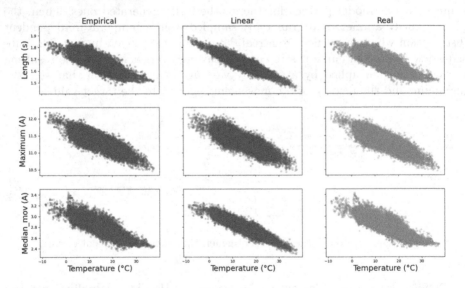

Fig. 3. Temperature dependence of three parameters (length, maximum and median of movement segment) for empirical method (left), linear method (middle), and real data (right).

Both methods have their advantages and shortcomings. The empirical method performs well when a lot of data is available, and poorly for few training curves. Additionally, the empirical method will naturally mimic the empirical distribution of the real data, hence making the generated curves arguably more realistic (Fig. 4). On the other hand, the linear method tends to overregularize, thus yielding a different feature distribution than the real data (see Fig. 3). However, through this implicit regularization, the linear method is able to extrapolate from few curves to a new temperature range, as discussed in Sect. 3.2. This makes the linear method attractive when few training curves are available. In addition, when outliers are already present in the parameter training data, the empirical method will reproduce them and abnormal curves may be contained in the synthetic data, too. This problem can be solved by filtering out statistical outliers before using the parameters for simulation. In contrast, the linear sampling method makes the assumption that the parameters used for curve manipulation follow a linear relationship to temperature and produces ideal distributions and curves. Note that a certain variation is naturally caused by measurement uncertainty related to the fact that the temperature measured at the relay house is only a proxy of the asset temperature.

Updating the Reference Curve. Synthetic curves can be generated by only using one reference curve per repositioning direction and a few samples of the real parameters length, maximum and median of the movement phase. Sometimes the typical shape of the current curves from a given switch can vary over time without this change being a critical development (e.g. slowly developing changes in track geometry), especially when looking at a long time-span or at a frequently used switch. When the objective is to replicate the current curves and related distributions for such a time-span, the synthetic curves benefit from an update of the reference curve after e.g. some fixed time interval. In practice, an update should be performed by a switch maintenance analyst when the reference curve begins to differ from real curves that are deemed normal.

Local vs Global. In practice, the temperature dependence of real current curves can develop over time. This is, the input parameters belonging to a narrower time span exhibit a lower variance per temperature bin than the whole parameter set and the slope and intercept of the linear regressions of the parameters in dependence to temperature slowly develop over time (see Fig. 7). This leads to the artifact that a randomly generated parameter set which used the whole available time span as training ("global") possesses a similar parameter distribution as the real data, but the parameter time series varies too much. Alternatively, linear regressions and variance estimations can be fitted for chronological data subsets ("local"), as is done in Sect. 3.1. This improves the parameter time series while the whole parameter distribution is still well represented.

3   Applications

In this section we illustrate the performance of our simulation machinery in two scenarios: 1. we generate data following the same distribution as in the given training data. And 2. we extrapolate from the training data to generate current curves at unseen temperatures. The performance of the simulation is evaluated in temperature windows of width $2°C$ using different quality measures.

3.1   Scenario 1: Replicate the Observed Distribution

We consider a two years long sequence of current curves corresponding to the blades movement in one direction of a switch (about 22.000 current curves). The challenge is to generate a new sequence of synthetic curves covering the same time interval. We present the results from the linear and the empirical methods as discussed in Sect. 2 in Fig. 3.

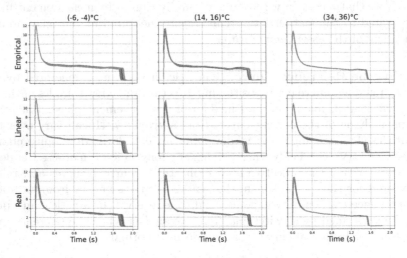

Fig. 4. Current curves generated by empirical (top) and linear (middle) methods, compared to real curves (bottom), in temperature range $(-6, -4)°C$ (left), $(14, 16)°C$ (middle) and $(34, 36)°C$ (right). The vertical axes show electric current measured in Ampere. In each temperature window we display 20 randomly sampled curves.

In a nutshell, we observe that the distribution of parameters is more realistic for the empirical method. We verify this in Fig. 4, where synthetic curves generated by the empirical and linear methods are compared with real curves in three temperature windows. Here, the linear method is seen to overregularize sometimes (see middle temperature window), while the empirical method yields visually correct results. This mirrors the intuitive recommendation to use the empirical method when plenty of training samples are available.

In Fig. 5 we compare the distributions (histograms) of several parameters obtained from real and synthetic curves generated by the empirical sampling method. Beyond the visual similarity, the p-value for the Kolmogorov-Smirnov test between the two distributions (see Chap. 14.2 in [6]) is shown, and indicates

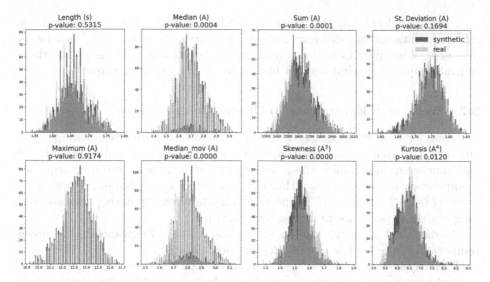

Fig. 5. Histograms of parameters from curves generated by the empirical method (blue) and from real curves (orange). The curves belong to the temperature range $(14, 16)°$C. (Color figure online)

that the distributions are indeed similar in a statistically rigorous sense. Similar yet slightly worse results are obtained for the linear method, as expected.

We compute another quality measure based on the Hausdorff distance. This is a well-known metric in mathematics that can be used to compare the geometry of quite general objects and sets. The Hausdorff metric provides a measure of distributional similarity. It does so by comparing individual points with an underlying metric, and then aggregating the individual distances into a global quantity (details can be found in Chap. 4 in [7]). Here, we want to measure the Hausdorff distance between the real and synthetic data. If we measured the distance directly, we would just get one number with no reference of whether it is big or small. We circumvent this problem by a bootstrap-type argument [8], that is by measuring the Hausdorff distance between several randomly sampled subsets of our sets, and then comparing the distances. Specifically, we randomly sample two subsets and measure their distance, and we do so in three different fashions: sampling both subsets from the real data (R), both from the synthetic data (S), and one from each set (RS). Each of these three distributions of distances can be plotted as a histogram, as done in Fig. 6. If the distances from the RS category are much larger than from the R and S categories, it means that the distances *between* the real and synthetic sets are larger than *within* those sets. In that case, we interpret the synthetic data to be significantly different from the real data.

On the other hand, if all three distributions of distances were identical, it would mean that it does not make a difference to sample from the real or from the synthetic set of curves, concluding that their distributions are similar.

Figure 6 includes the distribution of distances for both real and synthetic empirical data for two different underlying metrics (L^2-norm and Wasserstein distance). Both metrics indicate similarity between distributions in the three central temperature windows, but not in the extreme temperatures.

3.2 Scenario 2: Extrapolate to Unseen Temperatures

We consider a short sequence of curves in a limited temperature range, and our task is to generate a longer sequence with temperatures outside this range and time span. Specifically, the input consists of a three month long sequence (comprising winter and spring), thus the parameters span a limited temperature range (from −2.7 to 18.3 °C). The task consists of extrapolating the observed temperature dependence to unseen temperatures.

As discussed in Sect. 2, the linear method is able to extrapolate to unseen temperature ranges while considering only few data points.

Figure 7 shows a linear regression performed on the three input parameters derived from real curves (green points) and the generated synthetic parameters (blue points). We identify that the final distribution of the synthetic parameters is quite different from the real distribution, specially for extreme temperatures, but also regarding its overall shape. Still, the synthetic curves generated with those parameters are visually good, as shown in Fig. 8 for three temperature windows. However, we also see that some parameters of the synthetic curves are different from those of the real curves. This is due to the fact that the method does not have enough samples for all temperatures to "learn" the distribution correctly (see e.g. parameter length in Fig. 7) and that the slope and intercept of the linear regression obtained at the beginning of the time series do not hold for the following year and half (see e.g. parameter maximum).

In Fig. 9, we illustrate the real and synthetic parameters as a function of time, together with temperature. We observe that the parameter distributions

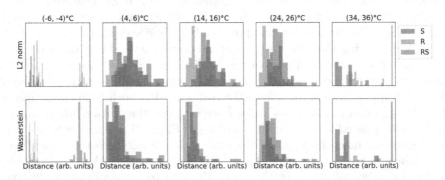

Fig. 6. Histograms of Hausdorff distances for subsets of the empirical synthetic data (blue), for the real data (orange) and between them (green), computed for different temperature windows and underlying metrics: L^2-norm and Wasserstein distance. (Color figure online)

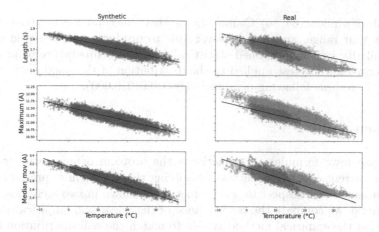

Fig. 7. Curve parameters as function of temperature for synthetic (left) and real (right) curves. The linear regression (black line) is computed with a limited amount of training curves (green dots) belonging to a small time interval and amounting to 15% of the real curves. (Color figure online)

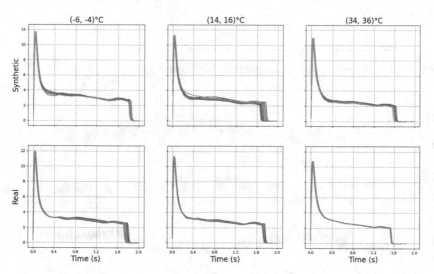

Fig. 8. Synthetic and real current curves from use case 2 for three temperature windows: $(-4, -6)°C$ degrees (left), $(14, 16)°C$ degrees (middle), and $(34, 36)°C$ degrees (right). In each temperature window we display 20 randomly sampled curves.

are generally similar in temperature ranges that span across training temperatures (winter period); especially for the parameter length, the real distribution for higher temperatures outside the training set is underestimated. In addition, performance decreases with time, especially for the parameter maximum. This presumably results from a long-term change in temperature dependence. Nevertheless, the similarity between curves in Fig. 8 is specially remarkable in the temperature window $(34, 36)°C$ since the synthetic method was not trained with curves in that range, and it is however able to produce quite realistic results. This similarity can be quantified statistically: in this temperature window, the Kolmogorov-Smirnov test applied to the distribution of the maximum, median and length, returns following p-values: $(0.003, 0.012, 0.000)$.

4   Discussion

In this paper we formulate and motivate the problem of generating realistic synthetic current curves. A method for solving that problem is presented, and its performance with respect to several metrics is shown in two scenarios. In the first scenario, we compare the performance of the linear and empirical method, finding that the empirical method is able to match the real distribution better. In the second scenario we only employed the linear method, since the empirical method is not suitable for that setting. Here we find that the linear method is able to generate realistic curves in unseen temperature regions, as shown in the third column of Fig. 8. In other words, the temperature extrapolation is performed well.

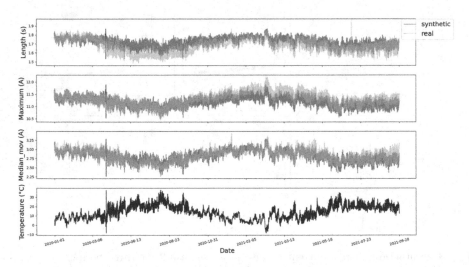

Fig. 9. Time evolution of three parameters: length (top), maximum (middle), and median of movement segment (bottom). The datapoints to the left of the vertical black line are the observed training data, as described in scenario 2 in Sect. 3.2. The synthetic datapoints are generated with the linear method.

Overall, we developed a method that can generate data from a complex distribution. Here we want to stress that, even though our method is applied to a very specific type of data (current curves with temperature dependence), the idea behind the method may be applied to other types of data, e.g. current curves with a similar structure from other applications. This opens up interesting possibilities for a general anomaly detection methodology in electromechanical systems. Since our method successfully generates synthetic current curves, it can assist anomaly detection models. Specifically, the method can be used to enlarge the training data of an anomaly detection model in order to cover rare situations (such as extreme temperatures) or even unseen conditions (as in Sect. 3.2 above). This can make anomaly detection models more robust.

It is an arguably difficult task to compare two sets of complex objects, such as current curves. We choose to split this task into two parts and consider several similarity measures. On one hand, we compare *individual* synthetic and real curves, and test whether they are similar (as in Fig. 4). On the other hand, we compare the two sets of curves *as a whole* by looking either at their statistical distributions (as in Fig. 5) or at their geometry (in terms of the Hausdorff metric, as in Fig. 6). One further similarity measure that could be used is an anomaly detection algorithm that is trained with the real data and then applied to the synthetic data. In that setting, the percentage of found anomalies ("false positives") would provide a good error measure.

There are further extensions of our work that we want to discuss. First, other interesting use cases can be considered. This includes the validation of anomaly detection methods, but also the retraining of an anomaly detection method after the switch conditions have changed (either by degradation or due to maintenance actions). Second, other generation methods can be used. We have presented what we call a parametric method, since the curves are reduced to a set of parameters that are modelled. Alternatively, one could use *nonparametric* methods, where the curves are generated as a whole. We have explored this idea using Generative Adversarial Networks (GANs) with good preliminary results, which offer an interesting and flexible alternative, although at the price of requiring more training samples. Another idea is to use dictionary learning to extract more accurate parameters, and then perform linear regression against temperature. Preliminary results show this to be a promising approach, as it automatically determines the dimensionality reduction to be performed, which can be useful when analyzing different switch types. And third, here we presented the generation of "normal" curves by modelling their temperature variation. In a future paper, we will discuss how to also generate synthetic abnormal curves related to different fault types and degrees of anomaly. These abnormal curves can be used to train anomaly detection methods in a better way.

References

1. García Márquez, F.P., Lewis, R.W., Tobias, A.M., Roberts, C.: Life cycle costs for railway condition monitoring. Transp. Res. E Logist. Transp. Rev. **44**, 1175–1187 (2008)
2. Innotrack (2009) Deliverable 3.3.2. Available sensors for railway environments for condition monitoring. https://www.charmec.chalmers.se/innotrack/deliverables/sp3/d332-f3p-available_sensors.pdf. Accessed 3 Jun 2022

3. Narezo Guzmán, D., et al.: Towards the automation of anomaly detection and integrated fault identification for railway switches in a real operational environment. In: Proceedings World Congress on Railway Research (2022). In press
4. Narezo Guzman, D., et al.: Anomaly detection and forecasting methods applied to point machine monitoring data for prevention of railway switch failures. In: Ball, A., Gelman, L., Rao, B.K.N. (eds.) Advances in Asset Management and Condition Monitoring. SIST, vol. 166, pp. 307–318. Springer, Cham (2020). https://doi.org/10.1007/978-3-030-57745-2_26
5. Vono, M., Dobigeon, N., Chainais, P.: High-dimensional Gaussian sampling: a review and a unifying approach based on a stochastic proximal point algorithm. SIAM Rev. **64**(1), 3–56 (2022)
6. Lehmann, E.L., Romano, J.P.: Testing Statistical Hypotheses, vol. 3. Springer, Cham (2005). https://doi.org/10.1007/978-3-030-70578-7
7. Rockafellar, R.T., Wets, R.J.-B.: Variational Analysis, vol. 317. Springer, Heidelberg (2009). https://doi.org/10.1007/978-3-642-02431-3
8. Romano, J.P.: A bootstrap revival of some nonparametric distance tests. J. Am. Stat. Assoc. **83**(403), 698–708 (1988)

AID4TRAIN: Artificial Intelligence-Based Diagnostics for TRAins and INdustry 4.0

Marcello Cinque[1,2], Raffaele Della Corte[1,3(✉)], Giorgio Farina[1,2], and Stefano Rosiello[3]

[1] Università degli Studi di Napoli Federico II, via Claudio 21, 80125 Naples, Italy
{macinque,raffaele.dellacorte2,giorgio.farina}@unina.it
[2] Consorzio Interuniversitario Nazionale per l'Informatica, M.S. Angelo, Via Cinthia, 80126 Naples, Italy
[3] Critiware s.r.l., via Carlo Poerio 89/A, 80121 Naples, Italy
stefano.rosiello@critiware.com

Abstract. Diagnostic data logs generated by systems components represent the main source of information about the system run-time behavior. However, as faults typically lead to multiple reported errors that propagate to other components, the analysts' work is hardened by digging in cascading diagnostic messages. Root cause analysis can help to pinpoint faults from the failures occurred during system operation but it is unpractical for complex systems, especially in the context of Industry 4.0 and Railway domains, where smart control devices continuously generate high amount of logs.

The AID4TRAIN project aims to improve root cause analysis in both Industry 4.0 and Railway domains leveraging AI techniques to automatically infer a fault model of the target system from historical diagnostic data, which can be integrated with the system experts knowledge. The resulting model is then leveraged to create log filtering rules to be applied on previously unseen diagnostic data to identify the root cause of the occurred problem. This paper introduces the AID4TRAIN framework and its implementation at the current project stage. Further, a preliminary case study in the railway domain is presented.

Keywords: Artificial intelligence · Fault model · Railway · Industry 4.0

1 Introduction

Diagnostic data logs are the primary source of data for understanding the behavior of a system. Diagnostic data logs are sequences of text lines -typically stored in log files- reporting on the runtime behavior of a system [3], including entries highlighting the occurrence of system failures. Their analysis has been extensively used for troubleshooting [2,7,19].

Root cause analysis is a well-established practice aiming at identifying the fault originating failures occurred during system operation. Understanding

© The Author(s), under exclusive license to Springer Nature Switzerland AG 2022
S. Marrone et al. (Eds.): EDCC 2022 Workshops, CCIS 1656, pp. 89–101, 2022.
https://doi.org/10.1007/978-3-031-16245-9_7

the fault underlying the occurrence of a failures is of paramount importance since it provides insights about the potential corrective actions to prevent failures from appearing later on and to avoid severe consequences [8], such as data and economical loss, damage to the environment. However, root cause analysis is often carried out in a manual fashion. Human experts generally rely on their experience to identify suspicious log entries, often by querying for predefined keywords. Understanding and traversing the diagnostic data logs from different components demands for substantial cognitive work by human experts. Highly specialized analysts are expected to face a number of challenges, which encompass the high volume and heterogeneity of data, the presence of different error and failure mode, the presence of corrupted, duplicated or redundant data, or even worst, the absence of data to infer the root cause of the occurred problem, the absence of consolidated and automatic analysis procedures.

This is especially true in the context of **Railway** and **Industry 4.0** domains, where smarts and control objects continuously generate high amount of diagnostic data logs. In these domains the root cause analysis is important to improve the reliability and safety of the operation. Complex systems like Train Control and Monitoring System (TCMS) [5] and smart manufacturing leveraging Industrial Internet of Things (IIoT) technologies [1] encompass a wide set of heterogeneous subsystems and components, each one generating diagnostic data logs. In addition, the presence of a fault typically leads to errors propagating through the system components, generating cascading diagnostic messages that increase the complexity of the root cause analysis and the cost of maintenance.

In this paper, we introduce the **AID4TRAIN** (*Artificial Intelligence-based Diagnostics for TRAins and INdustry 4.0*) project, which aims to support and improve the root cause analysis in Industry 4.0 and Railway domains leveraging Artificial Intelligence (AI) and data analytics approaches. The project purses the idea to bring together the system view provided by diagnostic data logs and the system expert knowledge, modeled as fault trees. AI and data analytics approaches are used to infer the fault model of the target system from historical diagnostic data in automatic way, which is then checked and integrated with the knowledge of system experts. The inferred fault tree model is subsequently leveraged to create log filtering and correlation rules to be applied on previously unseen diagnostic data to identify the root cause of occurred problems. The project is being developed by Critiware S.r.l. and an industrial railway partner acting as problem owner and data provider (Hitachi Rail Italy), and with the support of a national research center (CINI). The paper describes the concepts underlying the AID4TRAIN framework, its main components, and reports preliminary results obtained in a railway case study.

2   Problem Statement

Diagnostic systems available on modern train are able to automatically report information related to potential faults or functional anomalies. However, as anticipated, the consequences of a fault are hardly confined on the component that is first affected by the problem, and can have cascade effects (and related diagnostic messages) on many components. This leads to logs with an excessive number of lines which hardens the root cause analysis task, impacting to the overall life-cycle cost of a working train, due to the need of highly specialized maintenance staff. The analysis is impaired by several factors: data volume and heterogeneity, variety of fault types, presence of corrupted, redundant or repeated data, and, in rare cases, lack of useful information to reconstruct the event of interest. On the other hand, modern train supervision and control systems are equipped with more powerful computing resource, if compared to past systems, opening to novel opportunities to automate the on-board selective diagnostic task.

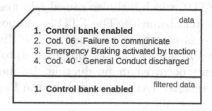

Fig. 1. Example of diagnostic log and filtering.

While there is still the need for human experts, to ultimately judge the hypothesized cause of a fault and program a maintenance action, the problem we aim to solve is to reduce the gap between the expert and the raw data, by providing a simplified view of knowledge automatically extracted from data in the form of fault trees. The challenge we address in this paper is to infer these models by mining potential correlations across huge volumes of data, spanning significant hours of functioning of the on-board equipment, in production environments. Learned grouping rules can be then used, in a later stage of the project, to automatically filter raw data on-board, hence reducing the amount of information to be delivered to the specialist, in case of anomalies.

As an example, a very common scenario pointed out by analyzing diagnostic data logs provided by the railway partner of the project is related to the *activation of a train control block*. When a train driver enables the control bank, typically a huge number of anomalies are reported into the diagnostic log. As shown in the *data* block of Fig. 1, this event (i.e., Control bank enabled) is recorded in diagnostic logs along with the cascading anomalies[1] (e.g., Cod.06-Failure to communicate, Emergency braking activated by traction, Cod.40-General Conduct discharged). The maintenance experts inferred that these cascading events are related to the activation of the control block (and then to the diagnostic systems not ready yet or still in startup phase), after time consuming manual analysis. Our framework aims to easy out this manual process by pinpointing only primary events (i.e., Control bank enabled

---

[1] Only a fragment of the log is reported due to space limitations.

in this example) and identifying secondary events (e.g., `Emergency braking activated by traction`), generating a data log where secondary events can be easily filtered out (as shown the *filtered data* block in Fig. 1) to easy out both operation and maintenance of the train system. Therefore, the aim here is to generate rules allowing to classify events in primary and secondary, through the analysis of historical diagnostic data logs collected during the system runtime.

3   Proposed Framework

The core of AID4TRAIN is a framework aiming to support smart maintenance processes by enhancing failure diagnostics. The core of the framework is a central *Fault-Tree Database* (FTD), which includes causal relationships between events occurring during the system behavior. The FTD is composed by a set of fault-tree models. These models are either provided by the diagnostics experts, by means of the *Fault-Tree Editor* (FTE), or proposed automatically by looking at past diagnostic events occurred in production, by means of the *Artificial Intelligence-based Log Analyzer* (AILA), as depicted in Fig. 2.

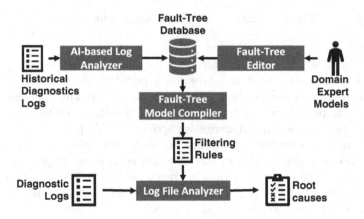

Fig. 2. AID4TRAIN framework components.

The FTE makes it easier for the domain expert to model well-known relationships between detected anomalies and possible root causes (e.g., from technical datasheet of the target system and its components). The AILA tool both identifies new failure modes and enhances existing fault trees by applying artificial intelligence algorithms to the historical field failure data logs. This component will automatically propose new fault trees to the domain experts. The expert can discover subtle fault chains leading to some system error that are not previously known. The tool can also propose new root events, in case a sequence of reported diagnostic events occurs multiple time in the same conditions but a root cause is not know. These discovered root events should be further analyzed by the experts and refined by means of the FTE tool.

The FTD stores all the relationship to effectively help both the system operators and the maintenance teams to quickly identify anomalies in all the diagnostics event produced by the system. To this purpose, another key component of the framework is the *Fault-Tree Model Compiler* (FTMC), which translates fault-tree models in log filtering rules. Those rules classify all the diagnostics events occurring during the system operation in either "primary" (e.g., the root cause) and "secondary" (e.g., the related propagating events). Diagnostic logs and filtering rules are imported and analyzed by means of the *Log File Analyzer* (LFA). This component analyses the set of anomalies reported in diagnostic logs, and it applies the rules given by the FTMC to point out automatically the possible primary causes of the events.

At the current project stage we are focusing on the design and implementation of the AILA component, which is presented in Sect. 4.

4   The AI-Based Log Analyzer

The Artificial Intelligence-based Log Analyzer (AILA) of the AID4TRAIN framework is a Python-based component, leveraging both temporal coalescence and unsupervised AI techniques to infer potential filtering rules. AILA implements the flow shown in Fig. 3, which encompasses the following three steps.

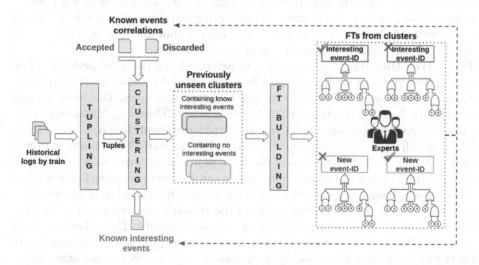

Fig. 3. The artificial intelligence-based log analyzer component.

Tupling. The event-tupling is a well-known technique [4] for temporal coalescence. A tuple is a collection of events that are close in time. The principle is due to the empirical observation that often multiple events that are reported together are due to the same underlying fault. Moreover, the same fault may persist, repeat often over time, and propagate to other components, which in turn may report an additional event into the log file. Two subsequent events are included in the same tuple if the time elapsed between the two occurrences is less than a fixed window size. Otherwise, they will be grouped in two different tuples. In this process the choice of the window size is a crucial factor, and represents a configuration of AILA. The obtained tuples are then represented by a binary sequence. Each element represent the presence of a particular event in the tuple.

Clustering. The AILA component assumes that the historical diagnostic data are not labeled (as in our railway case study), which prevents the use of supervised AI techniques. Therefore, in this step the tuples including a similar set of events are grouped together in a cluster leveraging an unsupervised AI technique, in order to learn a potential filtering rule. To this purpose we apply a hierarchical clustering technique based on single linkage [20]. To measure the distance between two tuples, we use the hamming distance, which is directly proportional to the number of different events occurred in the tuples. For each cluster we compute the number of events within the clusters, the probability of occurrence of the event within the cluster, and the average duration of the tuples within the cluster. Each cluster is considered to be a potential learned filtering rule if it contains at least two events and at least two tuples. Indeed, clusters with a single tuple are likely due to chance. Moreover, clusters with less than two events are not useful to learn potential correlations between events. The clustering step leverages a list of *known interesting events*, i.e., events that domain experts already known to be relevant in the target system, e.g., events representing root cause of failures. The clustering step leverages this list to divide the generated clusters in two groups: (i) clusters containing known interesting events and (ii) clusters containing no interesting events.

Fault Tree Building. Each cluster is transformed in a two-level fault tree. The root of the tree is the *primary event*, which is selected depending on the group the cluster belongs to. If the cluster contains an interesting event, this event is used as primary event of the tree, i.e., *Interesting event-ID* in Fig. 3; otherwise, the primary event is represented by a potential unknown event, i.e., *New event-ID* in Fig. 3, which needs to be investigated from domain experts. The remaining events of the cluster are used as leaves of the tree, representing *secondary events*. The inferred trees represent filtering rules, which can be summarized as follows: when all the events composing the fault tree occur within the related time window (i.e., the average duration of the tuples within the cluster), the root event of the tree is marked as primary, while all other events as secondary. This allows analysts to easily filter-out all the secondary events from diagnostic logs, focusing only on the primary ones when analyzing diagnostic data for root cause analysis.

Before considering the rules consolidated, the domain experts are expected to review the obtained fault trees. To this purpose each rule is translated in a XML standard representation of a fault-tree, which can further elaborated, discarded and accepted by a domain expert by means of a graphical fault-tree editor[2]. It is important to note that the reviews made by experts are provided as inputs to the

---

[2] We use FTEdit as fault-tree editor (https://github.com/ChuOkupai/FTEdit) and the Open-PSA Model Exchange Format as XML representation.

clustering step, which accepts the list of both *accepted* and *discarded* rules (in order to prevent that rules already analyzed by experts will be reviewed again). Further, if the experts identify new primary events during the analysis, they will be included within the *known interesting events* list. The accepted trees will be then provided to the Fault-Tree Model Compiler to translate the trees in filtering rules, which can be interpreted by the Log File Analyzer. As already mentioned, at this stage of the project we start addressing the design and implementation of the AILA component, and leverage an existing editor as FTE; FTMC, FTD and LFA components will be addressed later during the project lifetime.

5   Preliminary Case Study

As a preliminary case-study, we collected two weeks of diagnostic events logs related to a single train during operation by means of the train control room facility at our industrial partner. The collected dataset is not labeled; therefore, no information is provided about the relationship of the events.

Before providing the dataset to the AILA component, we execute a **data preparation** step, in order to transform the data in the format expected by AILA as well as to address suggestions provided by our industrial partner. First, the raw output of the diagnostic systems is converted in a table, containing for each event: a timestamp, the event-type and the event-code (which are described in the train model of the specific train), a description in natural language of the event and the name of the component affected. The obtained table is then analyzed to discard duplicated events (i.e., events with the same event-code and timestamp), according to the train control room team indications.

The dataset obtained after the data preparation step is composed by 57,653 events. In order to properly configure the AILA component, we first performed a sensitivity analysis in order to select the tupling window the AILA should use for the tupling step. Figure 4 shows the number of tuples by the selected tupling window. According to a previous study [4], a good tradeoff is represented by the knee point of the curve. Therefore, we obtained a tupling window of 5 s, corresponding to 5,744 tuples. The AILA component is then configured with the obtained tupling window, and it is executed on the prepared dataset. The clustering step performed by AILA generates 970 clusters. Only 348 clusters contains more than a single tuple, and only 249 contains at least two diagnostic events. Therefore, AILA considers the 249 remaining clusters as potential filtering rules learned in an automatic way, with a reduction of about 95% with respect to the number of tuples. Figure 5 shows the distribution of the number of events for each learned rule. The 70% of the total rules learned is composed by less than 5 events. Rules with more than 20 events represent only less than 7%.

In our preliminary study we also analyzed the effect of the tupling window on the number of potential rules obtained from the clustering step. Figure 6 shows that by varying the tupling window from 1 to 18 s, the number of potential rules ranges between 228 and 278, with an average of 253 rules, which is quite near to the 249 rules obtained with the selected tupling window of 5 s.

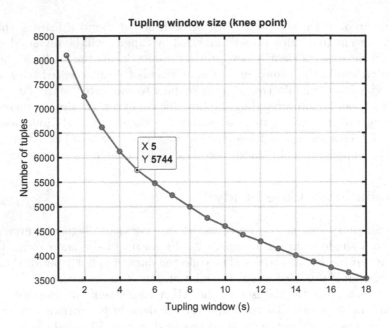

Fig. 4. Tupling windows size (knee point analysis).

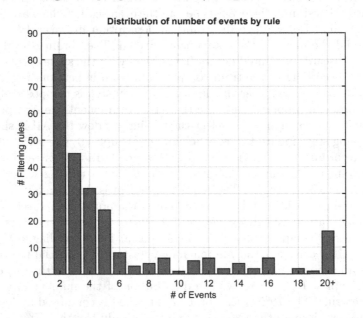

Fig. 5. Distribution of the number of events in each learned rule.

As indicted in Sect. 4, the resulting clusters are then converted in the Open-PSA fault-tree XML representation. As an example, the code fragment in Listing

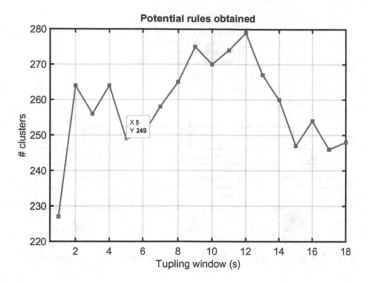

Fig. 6. Number of potential rules learned by tupling window selection.

1.1 and the corresponding graphical output in Fig. 7 show the tree representation of a rule inferred by a cluster, and which should be analyzed by a domain expert. To facilitate the analysis of the expert, each node of the tree (see Fig. 7) is enriched with the following information:

- an *eventID*, which is a combination of event name and event code extracted from the train model of the system, e.g., `017-_CloseIR_`;
- the *time window* (for the root event only), i.e., @window parameter, indicating the maximum time in which the rule applies;
- the *component* to which this event belongs to, i.e., @component parameter;
- the *probability* of occurrence, i.e., @probability parameter, which is defined as the ratio of number of times the event occurred in the cluster and the total number of tuples of the cluster;
- a natural language *description* of the event.

In the provided example, the cluster includes the events `017`, `019`, `VT_T2_4` and `VT_T7_4`, which have been grouped together by AILA. These events happened at least two times within a time window of 1.6 s. The event type `CloseIR` (`017`) has been indicated by the domain expert as a potential interesting event (through the dedicated list provided to AILA). Therefore, it has been placed at the root of the fault-tree. The obtained tree represented an example of rule obtained in an automatic way by using the AILA component, and that can be analyzed and modified by experts through the FTE component. In this respect, AID4TRAIN framework allows to obtain potential filtering rules from historical data in an automatic way as well as to combine the view provided by logs with the expertise of the analysts.

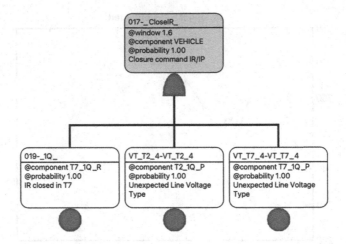

Fig. 7. Example of graphical representation of a learned rule.

Listing 1.1. Fault-tree XML Open-PSA Representation.

```
1  <opsa-mef author="AID4TRAIN">
2      <define-basic-event name="019-_1Q_">
3          <label>
4              @component T7_1Q_R
5              @probability 1.00
6              IR closed in T7
7          </label>
8          <attributes><attribute value="false" name="keep"/>
9          </attributes>
10     </define-basic-event>
11     <define-basic-event name="VT_T2_4-VT_T2_4">
12         <label>
13             @component T2_1Q_P
14             @probability 1.00
15             Unexpected Line Voltage Type
16         </label>
17         <attributes><attribute value="false" name="keep"/>
18         </attributes>
19     </define-basic-event>
20     <define-basic-event name="VT_T7_4-VT_T7_4">
21         <label>
22             @component T7_1Q_P
23             @probability 1.00
24             Unexpected Line Voltage Type
25         </label>
26         <attributes><attribute value="false" name="keep"/>
27         </attributes>
28     </define-basic-event>
29     <define-fault-tree name="471">
30         <attributes><attribute value="017-_CloseIR_" name="top-event
               "/></attributes>
31         <define-gate name="017-_CloseIR_">
32             <label>
33                 @window 1.6
34                 @component VEHICLE
35                 @probability 1.00
36                 Closure command IR/IP
37             </label>
38             <and>
```

```
39                    <basic−event name=" 019−_1Q_" />
40                    <basic−event name=" VT_T2_4−VT_T2_4" />
41                    <basic−event name=" VT_T7_4−VT_T7_4" />
42           </and>
43         </ define −gate>
44       </ define −fault −tree>
45   </opsa−mef>
```

6   Related Work

Event logs include empirical evidence about the errors occurred in a software system, hence, log analysis is efficient in classifying the propagation of errors and failure modes. Through heuristic tupling, the log errors are coalesced in tuples in order to associate them with a failure mode. For instance, error events occurring close in time are coalesced to represent a single failure mode. The validity of heuristic models for time coalescence in event logs is discussed by Hansen et al. [6]; their sensitivity analysis is also adopted in this paper. Spatial coalescence heuristics are adopted in the analysis of larger systems such as data-centers and supercomputers [9,15]. Collisions are the main issue of tupling heuristics: errors of different failure modes are associated to the same failure mode, for instance, due to the tuning of the time window or because the chance that independent failures occur on different nodes is not negligible. In this paper, the tupling heuristics are adopted to identify independent log events root causes. Once we get the tuples, we adopt the clustering to support the tuples.

Clustering techniques group the objects that are similar between them and dissimilar between the objects of other clusters. Clustering methods includes Hierarchical and Partitional clustering [21]. Partitional clustering defines at-priori the number of clusters, and searches the partition that maximizes a given function cost. For instance, k-means [12] tries to minimize the total intra-cluster variance at each iteration. Hierarchical clustering can be divisive or agglomerative. Initially, agglomerative algorithms assume that each cluster (leaf) contains a single object; subsequently, at each step, the "closest" clusters are joined to get a larger cluster. Measures of similarity between clusters are necessary to link the clusters. Linkage methods, such as Single-link, Average-link and Complete-link, calculate the inter-cluster distance considering all combinations of points between the two clusters [17,18], while geometric methods adopt geometric centers to represent the clusters, and to calculate the inter-cluster distance. For instance, the Ward's method is a geometric method which minimizes the intra-cluster variance. Divisive algorithms instead initially consider a partition formed by a single large cluster containing all the elements, and then divide it iteratively. Divisive clustering, as opposed to agglomerative ones, needs to measure the density or sparsity of points within a cluster to decide whether or not to proceed with the division.

Fault Tree (FT) is a well-known method to model the propagation of component failures in the system. FT is a tree, or more generally a directed acyclic graph, composed of one Top-Level Event (TLE, the root of the tree) and several intermediate events and basic events (the leaves). The events of an FT are linked though Boolean gates generating new intermediate events [16]. By describing the FT as Disjunctive Normal Form (DNF), each conjunction represents a cut-set, and each cut-set is a root cause of the TLE. Usually, the FT is adopted in FTA (Fault Tree Analysis) to qualitatively decompose the system failure in a hierarchical structure in order to identify the possible root causes as cut sets, or to quantify system dependability attributes. Building a fault tree requires a lot of manual effort, however, several studies discussed the possibility to build a fault tree from observational data making assumptions on the data set and conducting statistical tests [10,13,14] [11]. Nauta et al. [13] is the first completely automated tool to test the causality in the FT construction statistically.

We adopt the Fault Tree to model the filtering rules to detect the root causes in diagnostic logs. In that case, we are not interested in the accuracy of the fault tree in terms of a precise reproduction of the real hardware structure.

7   Conclusion

The paper described the key aspects underlying the AID4TRAIN project, which will provide Artificial Intelligence and data analytics approaches for supporting and improving the root cause analysis in Industry 4.0 and Railway domains. The paper introduced the software framework envisioned by the project, the design and implementation of its AI-based component, and a preliminary railway case. Future work will focus on the extensive implementation and validation of the AID4TRAIN framework in the context of real-world case study.

Acknowledgment. This work has been supported by the Meditech Competence Center under the AID4TRAIN Project (I65F21001010005).

References

1. Abuhasel, K.A., Khan, M.A.: A secure industrial internet of things (IIoT) framework for resource management in smart manufacturing. IEEE Access **8** 117354–117364 (2020)
2. Chuah, E., Jhumka, A., Browne, J.C., Barth, B., Narasimhamurthy, S.: Insights into the diagnosis of system failures from cluster message logs. In: 11th European Dependable Computing Conference (EDCC), pp. 225–232, September 2015
3. Cinque, M., et al.: An empirical analysis of error propagation in critical software systems. Empirical Softw. Eng. **25**(4), 2450–2484 (2020)
4. Di Martino, C., Cinque, M., Cotroneo, D.: Assessing time coalescence techniques for the analysis of supercomputer logs. In: IEEE/IFIP International Conference on Dependable Systems and Networks (DSN 2012), pp. 1–12. IEEE (2012)
5. Goikoetxea, J.: Shift2rail connecta: the next generation of the train control and monitoring system. Zenodo (2018). https://doi.org/10.5281/zenodo.1421620
6. Hansen, J.P., Siewiorek, D.P.: Models for time coalescence in event logs. In: 1992 Digest of Papers. FTCS-22: The Twenty-Second International Symposium on Fault-Tolerant Computing, pp. 221–227 (1992)

7. Kalyanakrishnam, M., Kalbarczyk, Z., Iyer, R.K.: Failure data analysis of a LAN of Windows NT based computers. In: Proceedings of the International Symposium on Reliable Distributed Systems (SRDS 99), pp. 178–187. IEEE Computer Society (1999)
8. Lal, H., Pahwa, G.: Root cause analysis of software bugs using machine learning techniques. In: 2017 7th International Conference on Cloud Computing, Data Science & Engineering-Confluence, pp. 105–111. IEEE (2017)
9. Liang, Y., Zhang, Y., Sivasubramaniam, A., Jette, M.A., Sahoo, R.K.: Bluegene/l failure analysis and prediction models. In: International Conference on Dependable Systems and Networks (DSN 2006), pp. 425–434 (2006)
10. Linard, A., Bucur, D., Stoelinga, M.: Fault trees from data: efficient learning with an evolutionary algorithm. ArXiv abs/1909.06258 (2019)
11. Linard, A., Bueno, M.L.P., Bucur, D., Stoelinga, M.: Induction of fault trees through bayesian networks. In: InProceedings of the 29th European Safety and Reliability Conference (ESREL) (2019)
12. MacQueen, J.: Some methods for classification and analysis of multivariate observations (1967)
13. Nauta, M., Bucur, D., Stoelinga, M.: Lift: learning fault trees from observational data. In: QEST (2018)
14. Nolan, P.J., Madden, M.G., Muldoon, P.R.: Diagnosis using fault trees induced from simulated incipient fault case data (1994)
15. Oliner, A.J., Stearley, J.: What supercomputers say: a study of five system logs. In: 37th Annual IEEE/IFIP International Conference on Dependable Systems and Networks (DSN 2007), pp. 575–584 (2007)
16. Ruijters, E., Stoelinga, M.: Fault tree analysis: a survey of the state-of-the-art in modeling, analysis and tools. Comput. Sci. Rev. **15**, 29–62 (2015)
17. Sneath, P.H.A.: The application of computers to taxonomy. J. Gener. Microbiol. **17**(1), 201–26 (1957)
18. Sørensen, T., Sørensen, T., Biering-Sørensen, T., Sørensen, T., Sorensen, J.T.: A method of establishing group of equal amplitude in plant sociobiology based on similarity of species content and its application to analyses of the vegetation on Danish commons (1948)
19. Tian, J., Rudraraju, S., Li, Z.: Evaluating web software reliability based on workload and failure data extracted from server logs. Soft Eng. IEEE Trans. **30**(11), 754–769 (2004). https://doi.org/10.1109/TSE.2004.87
20. Xu, D., Tian, Y.: A comprehensive survey of clustering algorithms. Ann. Data Sci. **2**(2), 165–193 (2015)
21. Xu, R., Wunsch, D.C.: Survey of clustering algorithms. IEEE Trans. Neural Netw. **16**, 645–678 (2005)

Railway Digital Twins and Artificial Intelligence: Challenges and Design Guidelines

Ruth Dirnfeld[1], Lorenzo De Donato[2], Francesco Flammini[1,3(✉)], Mehdi Saman Azari[1], and Valeria Vittorini[2(✉)]

[1] Department of Computer Science and Media Technology, Linnaeus University, Växjö, Sweden
[2] Department of Electrical Engineering and Information Technology, University of Naples Federico II, Naples, Italy
`valeria.vittorini@unina.it`
[3] School of Innovation, Design and Engineering, Mälardalen University, Eskilstuna, Sweden
`francesco.flammini@mdu.se`

Abstract. In the last years, there has been a growing interest in the emerging concept of Digital Twins (DTs) among software engineers and researchers. DTs represent a promising paradigm to enhance the predictability, safety, and reliability of cyber-physical systems. They can play a key role in different domains, as it is also witnessed by several ongoing standardisation activities. However, several challenging issues have to be faced in order to effectively adopt DTs, in particular when dealing with critical systems. This work provides a review of the scientific literature on DTs in the railway sector, with a special focus on their relationship with Artificial Intelligence. Challenges and opportunities for the usage of DTs in railways have been identified, with interoperability being the most discussed challenge. One difficulty is to transmit operational data in real-time from edge systems to the cloud in order to achieve timely decision making. We also provide some guidelines to support the design of DTs with a focus on machine learning for railway maintenance.

Keywords: Digital Twin · Railway · Artificial Intelligence · Machine Learning · Cyber-physical system · Internet of Things

1 Introduction

A Digital Twin (DT) is an accurate model of a physical entity which is kept alive at run-time and updated with real-time data collected from monitoring devices. DTs can be framed into general conceptual models including, among others, data collection management, model execution, and re-configurations planning [16]. The importance of the DTs is witnessed by the increasing number of ongoing standardization activities, such as the ones carried on by the ISO/IEC Technical sub-committee on IoT and DT[1], and the ISO/IEEE 11073 (Standardized DT Framework for Health and Well-Being in Smart Cities) [22].

In the railway sector, DTs can be used at different stages of the system life cycle and for different systems, including rolling stock (e.g., trains, trams, metros), signalling systems, infrastructures and manufacturing systems. They can be used to monitor physical assets, supervise train movements, provide information on passenger behaviour onboard trains, and detect or predict failures[2].

Several surveys are available in the literature covering different aspects of DTs. Semeraro et al. [34] conduct a systematic review on the DT paradigm in manufacturing enterprises. The authors discuss questions such as what a digital twin is, where it is used, when a digital twin has to be used and why, and what the challenges are when implementing a digital twin. Perno et al. [31] perform a systematic review on the enabling technologies and barriers of DTs in the process industry. Kaewunruen et al. [21] discuss DTs for railways with a focus on BIM (Building Information Modelling) applications. In the results, the authors argue that BIM demonstrates a strong DT potential for railway maintenance and resilience. Bao et al. [6] discuss the relationship and differences between DTs and traditional traffic simulation. Furthermore, the authors propose a three-layer technical architecture and analyse important technologies of DTs in traffic scenarios for intelligent transportation systems.

The purpose of our work is to provide a state-of-the-art and identify challenges and opportunities for DTs *in the rail sector* with a particular focus on maintenance applications and their combination with Artificial Intelligence (AI) techniques due to the potentials that this combination can bring to railway digitalization [17,35]. For example, DTs could be used to safely generate (synthetic) data related to assets' failures, by means of, for example, fault injection techniques [30], as to improve the performance of AI systems oriented at detecting possible defects/faults (e.g., [1]). On the other hand, AI could help to build more intelligent DT models [25] that could be used, for example, to understand how the physical asset would behave in case some parameters would change. In summary, in our view, DT and AI have the potentials to shift the current maintenance and inspection activities from scheduled and corrective to continuous and predictive.

The remainder of this paper is organised as follows. Section 2 briefly introduces the DT paradigm and related technologies. In Sect. 3, the results of the review are summarised. Challenges and open issues are discussed in Sect. 4. Section 5 provides some guidelines for designing a railway DT. Finally, Sect. 6 contains some final remarks and hints about future work.

2 Digital Twins

Several definitions of DTs exist [23]. In this study, we mainly refer to the definition provided by Bhatti et al. [8]: *"DTs concentrate on bilateral interdependency*

---

[1] https://www.iso.org/committee/6483279.html.
[2] https://www.globalrailwayreview.com/topic/digital-twins.

between physical and virtual assets". Their interconnection can be realised with IoT sensors that collect data and send them to the cloud. These data can, in turn, be analysed in the digital space by applying, among others, AI techniques (e.g., Machine Learning - ML - algorithms) and/or big data analytics [7]. Based on the results from the analysis, faults and anomalies can be detected or predicted. These features of a DT are shown in Fig. 1. Recently, the term *Cognitive Digital Twins (CDTs)* has been introduced, suggesting a potential development of the current DT paradigm toward a more intelligent, comprehensive, and full lifecycle representation of complex systems [25]. To achieve higher levels of automation and intelligence, cognitive capability is necessary, for example, to enable monitoring of unpredictable behaviours and autonomously developing dynamic strategies [42].

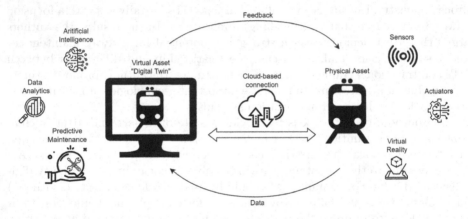

Fig. 1. Features of a DT, based on [8].

Recent technological advancements and innovations in the railway industry can support the adoption of DTs [31]. The relevant technologies identified during our review are the following:

- *AI techniques,* such as Machine Learning, allowing the DT paradigm to achieve its full potential.
- *Internet of Things (IoT) and Industrial Internet of Things (IIoT),* enabling seamless communication among devices. Sensors, RFID, NFC, actuators, etc., can collect massive amounts of data that can be further processed and analysed.
- *Virtual and Augmented Reality (VR/AR),* allowing users to better understand situations, and facilitating training and simulations in virtual environments.
- *High Computational Power,* enabling massive data processing, improved accuracy, and reliability, thanks to *cloud services* and lower hardware costs.
- *Communication technologies* (protocols, standards, MQTT, MTConnect, 5G and 6G networks, and others), enabling interoperability within IoT devices and proper data exchange.

- *Design processes*, including asset modelling and approaches ensuring decentralisation of DTs.
- *Development technologies*, including simulation, blockchain, virtual machines, etc. Simulation is a key enabler since it plays an essential role within DTs. Yaqoob et al. [39] argue that blockchain technology can reshape and transform DTs to ensure transparency, trust, safety and security.

3 An Overview of DTs and AI in Railways

We performed a literature review including about 60 papers addressing DTs in railways. The selected papers obtained via the literature review are categorised by year in Fig. 2. We then reduced the set to 25 papers specifically addressing DTs in combination with AI. We refer to the AI categories presented in reference [7], which are reported in Table 1.

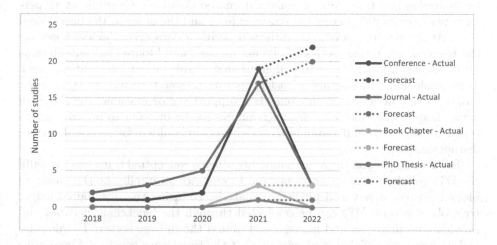

Fig. 2. Distribution of studies over the years and by publication type.

Machine Learning. ML applied to railway DTs mainly focuses on predictive maintenance [12,24,33].

Liu et al. [24] propose a framework enabling the application of industrial AI technologies for a Prognostic Health Management system for high-speed railways. The authors discuss the use of dynamic clustering of historical data for the identification of health conditions. Specifically, in a case study on traction motor condition monitoring, they discuss the use of an Artificial Neural Network for modelling the vibration between sensors that are close to the four wheels [24].

Similarly, Consilvio et al. [12] propose a generic framework and build a Decision Support System by combining ML, data analysis, and simulation techniques

Table 1. Mapping DT references to relevant AI categories.

AI Category	Literature works
Machine learning	[4, 10, 12, 13, 18, 19, 24, 26, 29, 33, 37, 38, 40, 41, 43]
Intelligent sensor data integration	[11, 15, 20]
Data mining	[14, 28]
Adversarial search	[2]
Computer vision and image processing	[5]
Evolutionary computing	[32]
Operations research	[27]
Other	[9]

for analysing real-time data to make automated decisions. Consilvio et al. perform two case studies, one at the strategic level and the other at the operational level. At the strategic level, the authors describe a data-driven model based on the K-means clustering method, Petri net models, and Monte Carlo simulations for decision support in order to evaluate a sustainable mix of interventions, such as renewals and refurbishments. At the operation level, Consilvio et al. describe a data-driven model based on a one-class support vector machine, the Bayesian network approach, and a linear programming model in order to improve maintenance operations and minimise costs caused by sudden failures and service disruptions [12].

Sahal et al. [33], on the other hand, introduce a conceptual framework to fulfil the DTs collaboration requirements and to enhance an intelligent DT based on blockchain technology and predictive analysis. By using the distributed ledger technology, several DTs can be connected through the blockchain network and provide data analytics and management across the railway sector. To minimise maintenance costs, Sahal et al. explain that the framework consists of predictive models that use data-driven ledger-based historical DT operational data and a distributed decision-making algorithm for improving the DTs collaboration. The authors argue that the framework can predict potential failures from rail-based operational data by applying ML algorithms and training the offline predictive model with this data. Then an online predictive model can be evaluated to predict the failures in railways. The outcome of these models serves as input for the consensus algorithm to make the best decision for data anomalies or to help decision-makers.

One of the most important issues in DTs development is their design and generation. Ariyachandra and Brilakis [4] argue that generating a DT of an existing railway from its Point Cloud Data (PCD) is a time-consuming and tedious task. Automation processes of this task face the challenge of detecting masts from air-borne LiDAR data since masts when scanned from above, are visible as thin lines. Thus, it is difficult to differentiate objects of similar shapes, such as signal poles, from masts. The authors propose a method that begins with tools that clean the PCD and identify its positioning, the resulting data sets are processed, and masts are detected using the RANSAC algorithm [4]. The article focuses on DT generation to save time and modelling costs; Ariyachandra and Brilakis propose a method for enabling the rapid adoption of a geometric DT.

Zhou et al. [43] introduce a DT framework for automatic train regulation and control with the goal of reducing train delay times and energy consumption. The authors achieve this goal by using a Convolutional Neural Network (CNN) to map the relationship between the train running time and the energy consumption of the speed profile and switch points [43].

Intelligent Sensor Data Integration. Jiang et al. [20] discuss the railway industry's demand for on-site data collection, control and management. The authors propose a monitoring platform design and architecture for intelligent high-speed railways. Jiang et al. also discuss the DT architecture, from collecting real-time data from the sensors, and integrating sensor monitoring data, to providing optimal solutions for failure handling. The aim of the DT is to develop a high-intelligence stage to intervene during abnormal working conditions through automatic monitoring and to prevent accidents.

Similarly, Errandonea et al. [15] propose an IoT approach for intelligent data acquisition for generating DTs in the railway industry, with the goal to create an onboard system for maintenance prediction in trains. The authors detail the architecture of the approach in three aspects: (1) The communication module for near-real-time communication and batch information transfer; (2) The functional design of the system, where the processing and integration of the sensor data are done in modules so that the system remains independent; (3) Data ingestion technologies, where the authors make use of Apache NIFI since it allows different data sources and parallel executions.

Data Mining. Du et al. [14] introduce a DT framework and its implementation method for urban rail transit. The proposed implementation method for the DT consists of four components, where: (1) the sensor network collects data; (2) onboard data is saved to a ground data storage device; (3) an analysis process is performed for mining and visualising data; and (4) AI algorithms are used for data mining, evaluating and predicting faults. The authors point out the necessity to pre-process the data by cleaning, integrating, transforming and reducing the data before the actual data mining process. For the analysis, the authors suggest using k-means when the labels belong to an unknown category, and for the classification of known data, they suggest using KNN, regression classification, neural networks, or naive Bayes.

Computer Vision and Image Processing. Avizzano et al. [5] introduce an algorithm for reconstructing rolling stocks from a sequence of images into an image model. The aim is to be able to generate DTs for complete rolling-stock vessels to serve for monitoring, diagnosis and failure prediction. The authors combine Kalman Filters, Gaussian mixture models and specific algorithms to track images of a train, which were taken by a fixed camera, so to provide a light and robust tracking system for image stitching [5].

4   Challenges and Open Issues

In this section, we summarise the most significant open issues and challenges to be tackled in the context of intelligent DT in railway applications in order to reach their full potential.

Interoperability. To enable DT to analyze and exchange data from heterogeneous systems in real-time, interoperability is essential. Dimitrova and Tomov [13] argue that current railway networks are managed by different tools and devices, resulting in unintegrated data, which makes interoperability and decision-making especially challenging. Sahal et al. [33] discuss the DT interoperability challenge and propose a data-driven ledger-based predictive model, which ensures intelligent and secure interoperability.

Connectivity. Sahal et al. [33] discuss communication technologies such as Beyond Fifth Generation (B5G) and 6G as opportunities for handling connectivity among the increasing number of smart devices in intelligent transportation systems.

Lack of Standards and Frameworks . Gan et al. [18], discuss the main challenges to develop standards for Industry 4.0 and achieve agreements in the goal to connect the entire supply chain and stakeholders.

Data Privacy and Security. Boockmeyer et al. [9] point out the importance of IT security and suggest the use of appropriate encryption techniques and software update strategy.

Scalability. In reference [33], the authors argue that blockchain technology is a solution for scalability since large amounts of DTs can work together in a hierarchical and granular manner.

5   Guidelines for DT Design

Based on the review findings, in this Section, we provide some guidelines for DT design with a focus on predictive maintenance, which is one of the most promising applications of DTs in railways. Figure 3 illustrates the workflow and necessary *tasks* to support DT design[3]. The main phases are: requirement specification, digital representation, data flow, conversion, analysis, decision process,

---

[3] Additional figures and tables from the conducted review, as well as an explanation table for Fig. 3 can be found in the GitHub repository: https://github.com/RuthDirnfeld/Replication-Package.

and validation. Each task includes several *steps* modelled by the nodes in the workflow diagram. The workflow was created based on the steps discussed in the primary articles by Liu et al. [24], Du et al. [14], Wagg et al. [36], Ariansyah et al. [3], and others.

Requirement Specification. The first task defines the purpose of the DT together with its expected benefits. Based on that information, the next step is to decide which enabling technologies are necessary for DT implementation.

Digital Representation. The objective of this task is to collect existing documentation about the physical asset and decide whether to automate the building of the DT or rather to model it manually. For example, Ariyachandra and Brilakis [4] generate a geometric digital twin (gDT) from its Point Cloud Data. Once this is decided, a visual representation such as 3D CAD models or a software of a simulated fashion of the physical asset is created.

Data Flow. The objective of the third task is to create the data flow. Different data can be collected, such as data on the position of the railway [14], the temperature of the motor [10], or the vibrations [13]. The position of the railway provides operational data, different weather conditions or humidity provide environmental data, and previously recorded data provides historical data. All three operational, environmental, and historical data can be sent to the data storage as input. There are two ways to store the data, the first is using cloud services, and the second is to store the data locally on a server with Internet access.

Conversion. This task addresses the design of the communication link between the physical and virtual assets. Depending on requirement specifications, for example, a 5G, B5G, or 6G communication technology could be selected. When implementing the design, it should be possible to transmit data between the physical asset and virtual assets. The next step is to process, clean and eventually reduce the data. Furthermore, it has to be decided whether the DT performs critical functions or not. When the DT is used in critical applications, it needs to be certified against relevant dependability and security standards.

Analysis. The fifth task is to create an analysis method, which depends on the expected benefits of the DT defined in the first task. In the analysis method, it is possible to choose whether to perform the analysis with, for example, supervised or unsupervised learning. Supervised learning algorithms are, e.g., neural networks [43], support vector machines or naive Bayes [12]. Unsupervised learning, such as the K-means algorithm, can be applied as an anomaly detection method [12].

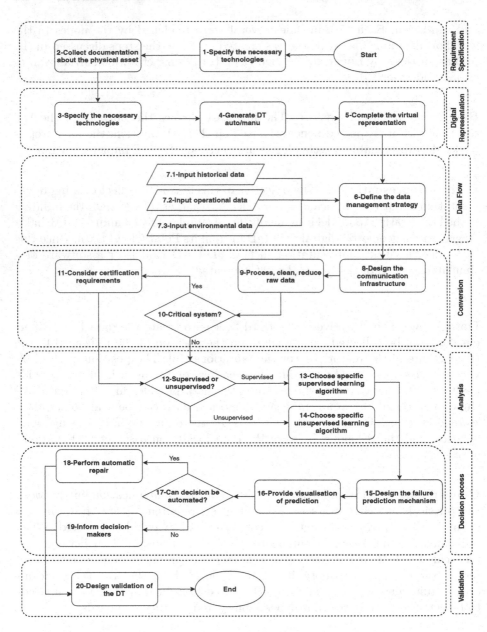

Fig. 3. Guidelines to implement a DT in a predictive maintenance example, based on the references [3, 14, 24].

Decision Process. Once the insight is obtained, the design of the decision process needs to be developed. The DT can be used to support human decisions, perform automatic repair actions, or assign tasks to the right personnel [24].

Validation. The last task is validation, where the designer has several design documents and models as an output of the flowchart. The validation can be done through the generation of a proof-of-concept.

6 Conclusions

In this paper, we have provided an overview of approaches related to the usage of DT in railway applications, with a focus on (C)DT and on the role of AI and ML as enabling technologies together with the IoT. We have highlighted some promising applications, design guidelines, as well as challenges to be tackled and future opportunities. Aspects worth investigating in future research have been highlighted that will allow building CDT fulfilling real-world requirements in terms of interoperability and trustworthiness. That will support several practical applications, especially for predictive maintenance, operational optimisation, and proactive safety.

References

1. Alderisio, F.: Manutenzione predittiva con matlab (2019). mATLAB Expo 2019
2. Ambra, T., Macharis, C.: Agent-based digital twins (ABM-DT) in synchromodal transport and logistics: the fusion of virtual and pysical spaces. In: 2020 Winter Simulation Conference (WSC), pp. 159–169 (2020)
3. Ariansyah, D., et al.: Digital twin development: a step by step guideline. In: 9th International Conference on Through-life Engineering Service (2020)
4. Ariyachandra, M.F., Brilakis, I.: Detection of railway masts in air-borne LiDAR data. J. Constr. Eng. Manag. **146**(9) (2020). https://doi.org/10.1061/(ASCE)CO.1943-7862.0001894. https://www.repository.cam.ac.uk/handle/1810/304356. ASCE
5. Avizzano, C.A., Scivoletto, G., Tripicchio, P.: Robust image stitching and reconstruction of rolling stocks using a novel Kalman filter with a multiple-hypothesis measurement model. IEEE Access **9**, 154011–154021 (2021)
6. Bao, L., Wang, Q., Jiang, Y.: Review of digital twin for intelligent transportation system. In: International Conference on Information Control, Electrical Engineering and Rail Transit (ICEERT), pp. 309–315 (2021)
7. Bešinović, N., De Donato, L., et al.: Artificial intelligence in railway transport: taxonomy, regulations and applications. IEEE Trans. Intell. Transp. Syst. 1–14 (2021). https://ieeexplore.ieee.org/abstract/document/9652066
8. Bhatti, G., Mohan, H., Raja Singh, R.: Towards the future of smart electric vehicles: digital twin technology. Renew. Sustain. Energy Rev. **141**, 110801 (2021)
9. Boockmeyer, A., et al.: From CCS-planning to testautomation: the digital testfield of deutsche bahn in scheibenberg - a case study. In: 2021 IEEE International Conference on Cloud Engineering (IC2E), pp. 258–263 (2021)
10. Boscaglia, L., Boglietti, A., andothers, S.N.: Numerically based reduced-order thermal modeling of traction motors. IEEE Trans. Ind. Appl. 57(4), 4118–4129 (2021)
11. Bustos, A., Rubio, H., Soriano-Heras, E., Castejon, C.: Methodology for the integration of a high-speed train in maintenance 4.0. J. Comput. Des. Eng. 8, 1605–1621 (2021)

12. Consilvio, A., Solis-Hernandez, J., Jimenez-Redondo, N., et al.: On applying machine learning and simulative approaches to railway asset management: the earthworks and track circuits case studies. Sustainability **12**, 2544 (2020)
13. Dimitrova, E., Tomov, S.: Digital twins: an advanced technology for railways maintenance transformation. In: 2021 13th Electrical Engineering Faculty Conference (BulEF), pp. 1–5 (2021)
14. Du, W., Zhang, T., Zhang, G., Wang, J.: A digital twin framework and an implementation method for urban rail transit. In: 2021 Global Reliability and Prognostics and Health Management (PHM-Nanjing), pp. 1–4 (2021)
15. Errandonea, I., Goya, J., Alvarado, U., et al.: IoT approach for intelligent data acquisition for enabling digital twins in the railway sector. In: 2021 International Symposium on Computer Science and Intelligent Controls (ISCSIC), pp. 164–168 (2021)
16. Flammini, F.: Digital twins as run-time predictive models for the resilience of cyber-physical systems: a conceptual framework. Philos. Trans. R. Soc. Math. Phys. Eng. Sci. **379**, 20200369 (2021)
17. Flammini, F., De Donato, L., Fantechi, A., Vittorini, V.: A vision of intelligent train control. In: Collart-Dutilleul, S., Haxthausen, A.E., Lecomte, T. (eds.) Reliability, Safety, and Security of Railway Systems. Modelling, Analysis, Verification, and Certification, RSSRail 2022, Lecture Notes in Computer Science, vol. 13294, pp. 192–208. Springer, Cham (2022)
18. Gan, T.H., Kanfoud, J., Nedunuri, H., Amini, A., Feng, G.: Industry 4.0: why machine learning matters? In: Gelman, L., Martin, N., Malcolm, A.A., (Edmund) Liew, C.K. (eds.) Advances in Condition Monitoring and Structural Health Monitoring. LNME, pp. 397–404. Springer, Singapore (2021). https://doi.org/10.1007/978-981-15-9199-0_37
19. Ikeda, M.: Recent research and development activities in maintenance technologies for electric railway power supply systems. Q. Rep. RTRI **61**, 6–10 (2020)
20. Jiang, R., Wang, W., Xie, Y., Yin, X.: Research and design of infrastructure monitoring platform of intelligent high speed railway. In: 2022 IEEE 6th Information Technology and Mechatronics Engineering Conference (ITOEC), vol. 6, pp. 2096–2099 (2022)
21. Kaewunruen, S., Sresakoolchai, J., Lin, Y.H.: Digital twins for managing railway maintenance and resilience. Open Res. Europe **1**(91), 91 (2021)
22. Laamarti, F., Badawi, H.F., Ding, Y., Arafsha, F., Hafidh, B., Saddik, A.E.: An ISO/IEEE 11073 standardized digital twin framework for health and well-being in smart cities. IEEE Access **8**, 105950–105961 (2020)
23. Liu, M., Fang, S., Dong, H., Xu, C.: Review of digital twin about concepts, technologies, and industrial applications. J. Manuf. Syst. **58**, 346–361 (2021)
24. Liu, Z., et al.: Industrial AI enabled prognostics for high-speed railway systems. In: 2018 IEEE International Conference on Prognostics and Health Management (ICPHM), pp. 1–8 (2018)
25. Lu, J., Zheng, X., Schweiger, L., Kiritsis, D.: A Cognitive Approach to Manage the Complexity of Digital Twin Systems. In: West, S., Meierhofer, J., Ganz, C. (eds.) Smart Services Summit. PI, pp. 105–115. Springer, Cham (2021). https://doi.org/10.1007/978-3-030-72090-2_10
26. Lumban-Gaol, Y.A., et al.: A comparative study of point clouds semantic segmentation using three different neural networks on the railway station dataset. Int. Arch. Photogram. Remote Sens. Spat. Inf. Sci. XLIII-B3-2021, 223–228 (2021)
27. Magnanini, M., Tolio, T.: A model-based digital twin to support responsive manufacturing systems. CIRP Ann. **70**, 353356 (2021)

28. Malek, N.G., Tayefeh, M., Bender, D., Barari, A.: Live digital twin for smart maintenance in structural systems. IFAC-PapersOnLine **54**, 1047–1052 (2021)
29. Milosevic, M.: Towards model-based condition monitoring of railway switches and crossings. Ph.D. thesis, Chalmers Tekniska Hogskola (2021)
30. Orive, D., Iriondo, N., Burgos, A., Saráchaga, I., Álvarez, M.L., Marcos, M.: Fault injection in digital twin as a means to test the response to process faults at virtual commissioning. In: 2019 24th IEEE International Conference on Emerging Technologies and Factory Automation (ETFA), pp. 1230–1234 (2019)
31. Perno, M., Hvam, L., Haug, A.: Implementation of digital twins in the process industry: a systematic literature review of enablers and barriers. Comput. Ind. **134**, 103558 (2022)
32. Ricondo, I., Porto, A., Ugarte, M.: A digital twin framework for the simulation and optimization of production systems. Procedia CIRP **104**, 762–767 (2021)
33. Sahal, R., Alsamhi, S., Brown, K., et al.: Blockchain-empowered digital twins collaboration: smart transportation use case. Machines **9**(9), 193 (2021)
34. Semeraro, C., Lezoche, M., Panetto, H., Dassisti, M.: Digital twin paradigm: a systematic literature review. Comput. Ind. **130**, 103469 (2021)
35. Tang, R., et al.: A literature review of artificial intelligence applications in railway systems. Transp. Res. Part C Emerg. Technol. **140**, 103679 (2022)
36. Wagg, D., Worden, K., Barthorpe, R., Gardner, P.: Digital twins: state-of-the-art and future directions for modelling and simulation in engineering dynamics applications. ASCE - ASME J. Risk Uncertainty Eng. Syst. 6(3), 030901 (2020)
37. Wang, X., Song, H., Zha, W., et al.: Digital twin based validation platform for smart metro scenarios. In: 2021 IEEE 1st International Conference on Digital Twins and Parallel Intelligence (DTPI), pp. 386–389 (2021)
38. Yang, J., Sun, Y., Cao, Y., Hu, X.: Predictive maintenance for switch machine based on digital twins. Information **12**(11), 485 (2021)
39. Yaqoob, I., Salah, K., Uddin, M., et al.: Blockchain for digital twins: recent advances and future research challenges. IEEE Network **34**, 290–298 (2020)
40. Zhang, S., Dong, H., Maschek, U., Song, H.: A digital-twin-assisted fault diagnosis of railway point machine. In: 2021 IEEE 1st International Conference on Digital Twins and Parallel Intelligence (DTPI), pp. 430–433 (2021)
41. Zhang, T., Du, W., Zhang, G., Wang, J.: Phm of rail vehicle based on digital twin. In: 2021 Global Reliability and Prognostics and Health Management (PHM-Nanjing), pp. 1–5 (2021)
42. Zheng, X., Lu, J., Kiritsis, D.: The emergence of cognitive digital twin: vision, challenges and opportunities. Int. J. Prod. Res. 1–23 (2021). https://doi.org/10.1080/00207543.2021.2014591
43. Zhou, M., Hou, Z., Liu, J., et al.: Digital twin-based automatic train regulation for integration of dispatching and control. In: 2021 IEEE 1st International Conference on Digital Twins and Parallel Intelligence (DTPI), pp. 461–464 (2021)

A K-Prototype Clustering Assisted Hybrid Heuristic Approach for Train Unit Scheduling

Pedro J. Copado-Méndez[1], Zhiyuan Lin[2]([⊠]), Eva Barrena[3], and Raymond S. K. Kwan[4]

[1] Universitat Oberta de Catalunya, Rambla del Poblenou, 156, 08018 Barcelona, Spain
`pcopadom@uoc.edu`
[2] Institute for Transport Studies, University of Leeds, Leeds LS2 9JT, UK
`z.lin@leeds.ac.uk`
[3] Pablo de Olavide University, Ctra. de Utrera, km. 1, 41013 Seville, Spain
`ebarrena@upo.es`
[4] School of Computing, University of Leeds, Leeds LS2 9JT, UK
`r.s.kwan@leeds.ac.uk`

Abstract. This paper presents a K-Prototype assisted hybrid heuristic approach called SLIM+KP for solving large instances of the Train Unit Scheduling Optimization (TUSO) problem. TUSO is modelled as an Integer Multi-commodity Flow Problem (IMCFP) based on a Directed Acyclic Graph (DAG). When the problem size goes large, the exact solver is unable to solve it in reasonable time. Our method uses hybrid heuristics by iteratively solving reduced instances of the original problem where only a subset of the arcs in the DAG are heuristically chosen to be optimised by the same exact solver. K-Prototype is a clustering method for partitioning. It is an improvement of K-Means and K-Modes to handle clustering with the mixed data types. Our approach is designed such that the arcs of the DAG are clustered by K-prototype and each time only a small fraction of the arcs are selected to form the reduced instances. The capabilities of this framework were tested by real-world cases from UK train operating companies and compared with the results from running an exact integer solver. Preliminary results indicate the proposed methodology achieves the same optimal solutions as the exact solver for small instances but within shorter time, and yields good solutions for instances that were intractable for the exact solver.

Keywords: Train unit scheduling · Hybrid heuristics · Clustering · K-prototype

1 Introduction

Many studies on passenger rolling stock scheduling in recent years have focused on Multiple Train Units (TU) which are the most commonly used passenger

S. Marrone et al. (Eds.): EDCC 2022 Workshops, CCIS 1656, pp. 114–125, 2022.
https://doi.org/10.1007/978-3-031-16245-9_9

rolling stock in Europe and many other countries, because of their well-known advantages over traditional locomotives/wagons such as formation flexibility, energy efficiency, acceleration and shorter turnaround times. A TU is a reversible non-splittable fixed set of train cars, which can be coupled/decoupled with other units of the same or compatible types if it is needed. Nonetheless, railway operators still have to face high costs associated with leasing, operating and maintaining their fleets. Hence, an optimal schedule of these TUs reduces operation cost. Given a daily timetable of trips, a fleet of several types of TUs, routes, and station infrastructure: Train Unit Scheduling Optimization (TUSO) aims at determining an appropriate assignment plan such as each trip is covered by a single or coupled units in order to satisfy the passenger demand [31]. Note that TUSO is an NP-hard problem as is proved in [7,33,39].

One way for solving the TUSO problem in the UK's railways is a two-phase decomposition framework [29,31], wherein the first phase the assignment of train units to trips is carried out ignoring some station layout details [31]. In the second phase, the fleet assignment is implemented taking account of station infrastructure to deal with shunting movements, unit permutation in a coupled formation and blockage of units, [28]. In this research we focused on the first phase. The aforementioned network flow level TUSO problem can be formulated as an Integer Multi-Commodity Flow Problem (IMCFP), which is based on a Directed Acyclic Graph (DAG) [7] representation, where the problem size is determined by the number of arcs. In [33], a branch-and-price method is designed to solve exactly small or medium-sized TUSO instances, but it is difficult to handle large instances due to its exact nature. In order to deal with this limitation, in [15] a hybrid heuristic approach called Size Limited Iterative Method (SLIM) is developed. In every iteration, the exact solver solves a reduced problems fast and comfortably, followed by an evaluation and modification of the arcs subset which is to be fed to the next iteration, such that the objective function will be no worse. Finally, the subset of arcs will converge to what is very close to an optimal solution. Local knowledge such as location, time, path of train connections in the DAG is used to decide which arcs are included in a reduced instance. For instance, arcs can be partitioned based on their time bands and in one particular iteration, all arcs from a band are included. This is referred to as "wheel rotation".

In this paper, we propose a novel approach for wheel rotation using K-prototype clustering. K-Prototypes is an upgraded version of K-Means [35] and K-Modes [21] suitable for mixed data types. It calculates the distance between numerical features using Euclidean distance (similar to K-means), but also calculates the distance between categorical features using the number of matching categories [22]. Based on their attributes, DAG arcs are thus grouped into clusters which are further used for creating reduced instances. This avoids explicitly using local knowledge to design strategies about which arcs to add in an iteration and thus the wheel rotation process is more generalised. Experiments based on real-world data from UK train operators show that the clustering-based SLIM often outperforms the exact solver and can even successfully solve difficult large instances on which the exact solver will fail within reasonable time.

The remainder of this paper is organized as follows. A literature review is provided in Sect. 2, next we formally describe the problem in Sect. 3. Our solving approach is presented in Sect. 4. This is followed by an illustrative experimental evaluation provided in Sect. 5 and by conclusions in Sect. 6.

2 Literature Review

2.1 Rolling Stock Scheduling

There are several variants of problems studied involving rolling stock (train unit) planning in the literature. [39] first formulates the rolling stock circulation problem (RSCP) as an integer multi-commodity flow problem on a single line with up to two train units that can be coupled. The objective is to minimize the number of units used. Issues such as train composition, attaching/detaching of units and unit blockage are not directly considered. A similar problem to [39] is studied by [4] and proposes an extended model where by introduce the concept of transition graph, unit orders in a coupled formation can be considered. [20] studies a variant RSCP where combining and splitting of trains are considered with a mixed integer programming model. [37] extends the problem scenarios of RSCP from a single line to multiple lines. Unit inventories are also described by extra decision variables. Branch-and-price is used to solve several real-world instances. The train unit assignment problem (TUAP) is first studied in [9], where it presents an integer multicommodity flow model. Since the maximum number of coupled units per trip is two, LP-relaxation can be enhanced in a precise manner with regard to the knapsack constraint [8]. Real-world instances of an Italian regional train operator with fleets of up to ten separate unit types and timetables containing 528–660 trains were solved. In [31], a two-phase strategy is presented for TUSO, in which the first phase allocates and sequences train trips to train units while temporarily disregarding station infrastructure specifics, while the second phase concentrates on completing the remaining station detail needs. In [33], a customised branch-and-price method for resolving the TUSO network flow level is given. Local convex hulls are utilised to enhance weak LP-relaxation bounds [32]. In [30], TUSO with bi-level capacity needs is investigated. In [28], station level unit conflicts are resolved by a feedback mechanism with added cuts. For larger and harder TUSO instances, a hybridized algorithm called size limited iterative method (SLIM) is developed in [12,16]. It explicitly uses local knowledge such as location and time band to create small instances and is able to solve difficult instances failed by the exact solver.

2.2 Hybrid Heuristics

The term of *Hybrid Heuristics*, or Hybrid Meta-heuristics [11,41] normally refers to a class of algorithms for solving challenging combinatorial optimization problems. In a narrower sense, however, hybrid heuristics can be described as a solution method in the following context: There is an exact solver available for solving the problem. However, due to the NP-hard nature of most combinatorial optimization problems, it can only solve small to medium instances. Therefore, an auxiliary heuristic method is developed to reduce the problem sizes in an iterative manner such that the small instances can be solved quickly and comfortably by the exact solver. In the early iterations, the solution quality from the reduced instances is often poor. However, the reduced instances are updated by customized search strategies in a way that in the final rounds of iterations most components needed for deriving optimal or near-optimal solutions will be included in the reduced instances.

A hybrid heuristic approach called PowerSolver is proposed in [26] for dealing with large and/or complex train driver scheduling problems. The relevant driver scheduling problems are solved by column generation [17] where a column represents a potential driver shift (duty). The corresponding set covering ILP model could have billions of columns, making the problem unsolvable. Power-Solver generates a series of tiny refined sub-problem instances that are fed into an existing efficient ILP-based solution. The usage of most relief opportunities (ROs, where/when a driver change can take place) is prohibited in problem instances, which reduces their sizes. A minimal collection of ROs is preserved in each iteration such that the following solution is no worse than the current best. A customized approach can help control the use of banned relief opportunities. It will also relax some of the restrictions placed on the problem instance before it is solved. PowerSolver provides a key step in fully automating the driver scheduling of UK train operators in large/complex real-world scenarios. It has been successful with many railway companies and has been routinely used as a key component of TrainTRACS, a commercial crew scheduling software suite [25]. A general hybrid metaheuristic method named Construct, Merge, Solve & Adapt (CMSA) is proposed by [6] for solving combinatorial optimization problems. CMSA generates a smaller sub-instance of the problem, which has a solution that is also feasible to its parent problem. A high quality solution is obtained by iteratively applying an exact solver to the reduced sub-instances. Strategies are designed such that feedback based on the results of the exact solver in a previous iteration will be provided to guide the parameter settings in next iteration. The effectiveness of CMSA was tested by two exemplar problems: the minimum common string partition problem and the minimum covering arborescence problem. From the experiment results, it is demonstrated that CMSA can achieve similar performance compared to the exact solver for small to medium sized instances, while its performance is significantly better than the exact solver when it came to large instances. See [3, 5, 18, 19] for recent research using CMSA.

2.3   K-Prototype Clustering

K-Prototype was first proposed in [22], which combines K-Means (for numerical data) [34, 35] and K-Modes (for categorical data) [21]. The part for clustering categorical data was later improved by [10]. K-Prototype is able to cluster data of mixed types. Assume there are two mixed-type objects X and Y described by their attributes $A_1^r, A_2^r, \ldots, A_p^r, A_{p+1}^c, \ldots, A_m^c$ (the fist p attributes are numerical and the remaining $m - p$ are categorical). Let x_j and y_j be the value of the j-th attribute of X and Y respectively. The distance between X and Y is measured by

$$d(X,Y) = \sum_{j=1}^{p}(x_j - y_j)^2 + \gamma \sum_{j=p+1}^{m} \delta(x_j, y_j). \tag{1}$$

The first term is the (squared) Euclidean distance on numeric attributes while the second is a simple matching dissimilarity measure on the categorical attributes, i.e. $\delta(x_j, y_j) = 0$ if $x_j = y_j$ (same category) and $\delta(x_j, y_j) = 1$ otherwise. Weight γ is used to adjust the importance of the two types of attributes. Suppose the target number of clusters is given by $K > 0$, and there are n objects, the goal is to find the attribute values of each "centrtoid" of cluster l for attribute j, denoted by q_{lj} and whether an object i belongs to cluster l or not, indicated by binary variables $w_{il} \in \{0,1\}, 1 \leq i \leq n, 1 \leq l \leq K$ such that the total distance is minimised by [22].

$$\min_{w,q} \sum_{l=1}^{K} \left(\sum_{i=1}^{n} w_{il} \sum_{j=1}^{p}(x_{ij} - q_{lj})^2 + \gamma \sum_{i=1}^{n} w_{il} \sum_{j=p+1}^{m} \delta(x_{ij}, q_{lj}) \right) \tag{2}$$

subject to

$$\sum_{l=1}^{K} w_{il} = 1, \quad 1 \leq i \leq n. \tag{3}$$

The appropriate number of clusters K can be determined by the "elbow method" [24]. For the recent development of algorithms for clustering data with mixed type, see surveys [2, 38].

As a kind of machine learning algorithm for processing data, K-Prototype has been applied in various data science research, most of which are out of the scope of our paper. Apart from data science, there are a few cases where K-Prototype is used for applied problems. In [23], it assists optimising pavement lifecycle planning. [27] applies K-Prototype for the identification and analysis of vulnerable populations for malaria. In [40], K-Prototype has been applied in detecting anomaly intrusion activities. As far as the authors are aware, no application of K-Prototype has been used in improving optimisation algorithms for railway planing and management problems.

3   Problem Description

Train unit scheduling optimization (TUSO) concerns the assignment of train units to cover all the trips for an operational day, aiming at using the minimum number of train units while reducing the operational cost. It also allows the possibility of coupling and decoupling activities to achieve optimal use [31].

Our approach transforms the background problem TUSO into an Integer Multi-commodity Flow Problem (IMCFP) based on an initial DAG $\mathcal{G} = (\mathcal{N}, \mathcal{A})$, where the set $\mathcal{N}$ contains all the nodes (trips and sign-on/off nodes) and the set $\mathcal{A}$ contains all feasible arcs (feasible connections between nodes). Figure 1 illustrates a sample instance of five trips. More specifically, the node set $\mathcal{N} = \mathcal{N}_0 \bigcup \{s, s'\}$, where $\mathcal{N}_0$ represents the set of trips, and s and s' the *source* and *sink* nodes, respectively. Beside, each node is labelled with station origin/destination and also departure/arrival time. The arc set is defined as $\mathcal{A} = \mathcal{A}' \bigcup \mathcal{A}_0$, where $\mathcal{A}' = \{(i, j) | i, j \in \mathcal{N}\}$ is the *connection-arc* set and $\mathcal{A}_0 = \{(s, j) | j \in \mathcal{N}\} \cup \{(j, s') | j \in \mathcal{N}\}$ is the *sign-on/off* arc set. Each arc (i, j) stands for the potential linkage relation between trip i and trip j to be served by the same TU at the same station (same-location arc) or different stations (empty-running arc). Observe that the dashed arrow in Fig. 1 represents an empty running arc.

Moreover, each arc a is labelled with the slack time a_t, which corresponds to the difference between the trip departure time of the successor node and the trip arrival time of the predecessor node, and cost a_c, which is defined by the waiting or empty running time between two trips linked by a. In the case of empty running arcs, the cost also considers the mileage. Finally, an $s - s'$ path in $\mathcal{G}$ represents a sequenced daily workload (the train nodes in the path in $\mathcal{G}$) for a possible unit schedule or diagram and the flow on it indicates the number of units used for serving those trains. The set of commodities K represents the set of TU types allowed. Note that a solution of IMCFP is a sub-graph of $\mathcal{G}$ such that all nodes are connected by paths from $s - s'$. Therefore, the optimal solution is the most *compact* sub-graph of $\mathcal{G}$, where compact refers to one minimum-cost subgraph. More details about the IMCFP and the DAG representation can be found in [33].

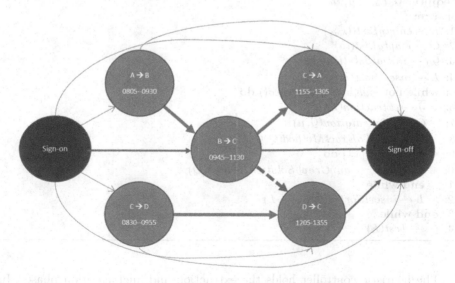

Fig. 1. Example of the initial DAG for an instance with five trips

4   Methodology

The proposed methodology is based on the hybridization technique introduced in [12,13]. This methodology relies on the iterative resolution of sub-instances of the original graph instance $\mathcal{G}$. In each iteration, from a graph solution or *Essential Graph* $\overline{\mathcal{G}}$, which is characterised by containing an *Essential* number of arcs, an *Augmented Graph* $\widehat{\mathcal{G}}$ is constructed by extending the $\overline{\mathcal{G}}$ up to a fraction μ of $\mid A(\mathcal{G}) \mid$ in such way that $\mid \mathcal{A}(\overline{\mathcal{G}}) \mid < \mid \mathcal{A}(\widehat{\mathcal{G}}) \mid \ll \mid \mathcal{A}(\mathcal{G}) \mid$. Therefore, solving the problem on $\widehat{\mathcal{G}}$ yields a graph solution $\overline{\mathcal{G}}'$ which will be at least as good as $\overline{\mathcal{G}}$ and, after few iterations, it is expected to reach high-quality (sub-)optimal solutions in reasonable time.

The general SLIM+KP algorithm is described in the following and pseudo-coded in Algorithm 1. This requires the following input parameters: stopping criteria; l_{max}, that stands for the size of ranked solutions list; the aforementioned augmentation rate μ; and th, that is the number of sub-problems concurrently solving. The main loop works as follows: an initial feasible solution $\overline{\mathcal{G}}_0$ is inserted in the list of ranked solutions in lines 3–4 of Algorithm 1. The initial solution is constructed based on a first-in-first-out (FIFO) greedy heuristic [20,36]. During the extraction phase of each iteration (lines 5–10), the algorithm randomly chooses an incumbent solution $\overline{\mathcal{G}}$ from the ranked list L. Then the algorithm produces $\widehat{\mathcal{G}}$ (augmentation phase), which is sent to exact method [33] to be solved. The exact solver yields a solution graph $\overline{\mathcal{G}}'$ and the algorithm iterates until one stopping criterion is satisfied.

Algorithm 1. SLIM+KP

Require: $\mathcal{G}, l_{max}, \mu, th$
Ensure: $\mathcal{G}^*$
 1: $L \leftarrow emptyList(l_{max})$
 2: $Q \leftarrow emptyList(th)$
 3: $\overline{\mathcal{G}}_0 \leftarrow initialSolution(\mathcal{G})$
 4: $L \leftarrow insertSorted(\langle \overline{\mathcal{G}}^0 \rangle, L)$
 5: **while not** $endCriteriaReached()$ **do**
 6:    $\overline{\mathcal{G}} \leftarrow extraction(L)$
 7:    $\widehat{\mathcal{G}} \leftarrow augmentation(\overline{\mathcal{G}}, \mu)$
 8:    $Q \leftarrow sendToExactMethod(Q, \widehat{\mathcal{G}})$
 9:    **while** $th = \mid Q \mid$ **do**
10:       $\langle \overline{\mathcal{G}}'_1, \ldots \rangle \leftarrow anyGraphSolutionReady?(Q)$
11:    **end while**
12:    $L \leftarrow insertSorted(\langle \overline{\mathcal{G}}'_1, \ldots \rangle, L)$
13: **end while**
14: $\overline{\mathcal{G}}^* \leftarrow best(L)$

The heuristic controller holds the extraction and augmentation phases. In the extraction, the incumbent $\overline{\mathcal{G}}$ is chosen from the solution list L. This action can be carried out using a solution randomly chosen overall graph solutions uniformly distributed in L. Regarding the augmentation phase, the augmented graph $\widehat{\mathcal{G}} = (\widehat{\mathcal{N}}, \widehat{\mathcal{A}})$ is built by setting the set $\widehat{\mathcal{N}}$ equal to set $\overline{\mathcal{N}}$ and the arc set $\widehat{\mathcal{A}} = \overline{\mathcal{A}} \cup \mathcal{H}$ is extended by means of the set $\mathcal{H} \subset \mathcal{A}$; as mentioned before, this set $\mid \mathcal{H} \mid$ is limited by the $\mu \cdot \mid \mathcal{A}(\mathcal{G}) \mid$. The set $\mathcal{H}$ is formed using a designed arc selection operator applied on arc clusters. This operator starts by selecting a random cluster in the first step, and collecting the arcs from this cluster as *circular* list in the second step. The construction of the clusters was carried out using K-Prototype methodology [22], which is carried out before executing the algorithm. As mentioned in Sect. 2.3, K-Prototype is a clustering method to deal with mixed data types. We have used the attributes contained in each arc to create the clusters. The description of these attributes is included in Table 1. Recall that each arc $v = (A, B)$ that links two trips A and B represents that the train units of trip A will also perform trip B.

Table 1. Summary of the arc attributes used by K-Prototypes method for a given arc (A, B) between trips A and B. "C": categorical, "N": numerical.

Attribute	Description	Type
id_A	Identifier of trip A	C
loc_A	Location of arrival trip A	C
arr_A	Arrival time of trip A to loc_A	N
ban_A	"true" if location loc_A is banned for coupling/decoupling operations, o/w "false"	C
id_B	Identifier of trip B	C
loc_B	Location of departure trip B	C
dep_B	Departure time of trip B from loc_B	N
ban_B	"true" if location loc_B is banned for coupling/decoupling operations, o/w "false"	C
$slacktime$	Difference between arr_A - dep_B	N

5   Computational Experiments

To check the effectiveness of the proposed K-prototype assisted hybrid methodology, we have solved several instances from the data set described in [14], and we have compared our results with those obtained with the standalone exact method [33]. These instances differ in the number of nodes, arcs and fleet size. In order to solve each instance, we first create a partition of its arc set. For this purpose, we use the previously mentioned K-Prototype method [22]. In addition, to determine the optimal number of clusters, we have used the elbow method on the cost function provided by this method. Second, the instances are solved with the exact method within a maximum time of 2 hours. Finally, we repeat each experiment with SLIM, considering the previously generated clusters as heuristic arc-selection operators, and setting the stopping criteria to the maximum time of 30 min. Regarding software, the exact method has been implemented in Mosel 3.0 and uses the Xpress MP 7.9 solver. SLIM has been developed in C#, while the K-Prototype method was included in the Python 3.6 module `kmodes` [1]. All the experiments have been performed on a computer with Windows Home 11, CPU Intel(R) i7-8750H and 16 GB of RAM memory.

Results are shown in Table 2, which contains the following information for each instance. The first column refers to the instance name, which include the number of nodes and arcs (node#_arc#_type#). Second and third columns refer to the results obtained by the exact method and indicate the objective function value and the fleet size, respectively. Finally, the last three columns present the results obtained with the proposed K-prototype assisted hybrid methodology, indicating the number of clusters, the objective function, and the resulting fleet size. Observe that, for the cases where the exact solver achieves optimal solutions, the proposed hybrid methodology yields the same optimal objective values, and SLIM+KP is able to yield solutions for instances that are intractable for the exact solver.

Table 2. Computational results from SLIM+K-Prototype and exact solver (exact solver ran for 120 min and SLIM+KP ran for 30 min)

Instance	Exact method		SLIM +K-Prototype		
	Obj.	Fleet	#Clusters	Obj.	Fleet
499_20151_2	–	–	4	85.747	85
510_2708_2	–	–	4	154.68	152
100_2164_1	19.412	18	4	19.412	18
358_3871_2	44.302	44	4	44.302	44

6   Conclusions and Future Research

We have presented a K-Prototype assisted hybrid heuristic approach SLIM+KP to solve large instances of the Train Unit Scheduling Optimization problem. This problem can be modelled as an IMCFP based on a DAG, where each node represent a train trip and each arc (i, j) stands for the potential linkage relation between trip i and trip j to be served by the same train unit. For a fixed number of nodes, the higher the number of arcs, the higher the complexity of the problem. In order to solve large size instances, our hybrid methodology iteratively reduces the number arcs of the initial DAG and solve the problem based on the reduced graph by the exact method presented in [33]. The arc set is partitioned by means of the K-Prototype, a clustering method that can handle mixed data. This partition will then be the basis of the proposed K-Prototype assisted hybrid heuristic approach since arcs are selected depending on the cluster they belong to. By performing computational experiments on real-world cases from UK train operating companies, we have compared our hybrid implementation against the exact solver [33]. The methodology has succeeded in achieving the same optimal solutions for small instances that could be solved exactly but with only about a quarter of time, and yields good solutions for instances that were intractable for the exact solver.

Future research includes more sophisticated strategies in SLIM+KP and to extend the applied cases to even larger real-world instances. We are also interested in further proposing an even more generalised approach for partitioning solution space (wheel rotation) for hybrid heuristics based on clustering and other methodological/algorithmic methods.

Acknowledgements. We would like to thank Greater Anglia, Great Western Railway, Northern and Tracsis plc for supporting us with data for our research. This work was partly supported by grants PID2019-106205GB-I00, PID2019-104263RB-C41, and UPO-1263769. This support is gratefully acknowledged.

References

1. Kmodes. https://pypi.org/project/kmodes/
2. Ahmad, A., Khan, S.S.: Survey of state-of-the-art mixed data clustering algorithms. IEEE Access **7**, 31883–31902 (2019)
3. Akbay, M., Blum, C.: Application of CMSA to the minimum positive influence dominating set problem, vol. 339, pp. 17–26 (2021)
4. Alfieri, A., Groot, R., Kroon, L., Schrijver, A.: Efficient circulation of railway rolling stock. Transp. Sci. **40**(3), 378–391 (2006)
5. Blum, C., Blesa, M.J.: A comprehensive comparison of metaheuristics for the repetition-free longest common subsequence problem. J. Heuristics **24**(3), 551–579 (2017). https://doi.org/10.1007/s10732-017-9329-x
6. Blum, C., Pinacho, P., López-Ibáñez, M., Lozano, J.A.: Construct, merge, solve and adapt a new general algorithm for combinatorial optimization. Comput. Oper. Res. **68**, 75–88 (2016)
7. Cacchiani, V., Caprara, A., Toth, P.: Solving a real-world train-unit assignment problem. Math. Program. **124**(1–2), 207–231 (2010)
8. Cacchiani, V., Caprara, A., Maróti, G., Toth, P.: On integer polytopes with few nonzero vertices. Oper. Res. Lett. **41**(1), 74–77 (2013)
9. Cacchiani, V., Caprara, A., Toth, P.: Scheduling extra freight trains on railway networks. Transp. Res. Part B Methodol. **44**(2), 215–231 (2010)
10. Cao, F., Liang, J., Bai, L.: A new initialization method for categorical data clustering. Expert Syst. Appl. **36**, 10223–10228 (2009)
11. Christian Blum, G.R.: Hybrid Metaheuristics: Powerful Tools for Optimization. Springer, Cham (2016). https://doi.org/10.1007/978-3-319-30883-8
12. Copado-Mendez, P., Lin, Z., Kwan, R.: Size limited iterative method: a hybridized heuristic for train unit scheduling optimization. In: CASPT 2018 (2017)
13. Copado-Mendez, P., Lin, Z., Kwan, R.: Size limited iterative method (slim) for train unit scheduling (2017)

14. Copado-Mendez, P.J., Lin, Z., Kwan, R.S.K.: Train units scheduling optimization (2018). http://archive.researchdata.leeds.ac.uk/id/eprint/537
15. Copado-Mendez, P.J., Lin, Z., Kwan, R.S.: Size limited iterative method (SLIM) for train unit scheduling. In: Proceedings of the 12th Metaheuristics International Conference, Barcelona, Spain (2017). Leeds (2017)
16. Copado-Mendez, P., Lin, Z., Kwan, R.: Size limited iterative method (SLIM) for train unit scheduling. In: Proceedings of the 12th Metaheuristics International Conference, Barcelona, Spain (2017)
17. Desrosiers, J., Lubbecke, M.: A Primer in Column Generation, pp. 1–32, March 2006
18. Dupin, N., Talbi, E.G.: Matheuristics to optimize refueling and maintenance planning of nuclear power plants. J. Heuristics **27**, 63–105 (2021)
19. Ferrer, J., Chicano, F., Ortega-Toro, J.: Cmsa algorithm for solving the prioritized pairwise test data generation problem in software product lines. J. Heuristics **27**, 1–21 (2021)
20. Fioole, P.J., Kroon, L., Maróti, G., Schrijver, A.: A rolling stock circulation model for combining and splitting of passenger trains. Eur. J. Oper. Res. **174**, 1281–1297 (2006)
21. Huang, Z.: Clustering large data sets with mixed numeric and categorical values. In: The First Pacific-Asia Conference on Knowledge Discovery and Data Mining, pp. 21–34 (1997)
22. Huang, Z.: Extensions to the k-means algorithm for clustering large data sets with categorical values. Data Min. Knowl. Disc. **2**(3), 283–304 (1998)
23. Karimzadeh, A., Sabeti, S., Shoghli, O.: Optimal clustering of pavement segments using k-prototype algorithm in a high-dimensional mixed feature space. J. Manag. Eng. **37**(4), 04021022 (2021)
24. Koelbel, C.H., Loveman, D.B., Schreiber, R.S., Steele, G.L., Zosel, M.E.: Using MPI-2 PVM: parallel virtual machine-a users' guide and tutorial for network parallel computing. Schauble, C.J.C., Domik, G. (eds.) Unstructured Scientific Computation on Scalable Multiprocessors (1991)
25. Kwan, R.: Case studies of successful train crew scheduling optimisation. J. Sched. **14**, 423–434 (2011)
26. Kwan, R., Kwan, A.: Effective search space control for large and/or complex driver scheduling problems. Ann. Oper. Res. **155**, 417–435 (2007)
27. Li, C., et al.: Identification and analysis of vulnerable populations for malaria based on k-prototypes clustering. Environ. Res. **176**, 108568 (2019)
28. Li, L., Kwan, R., Lin, Z., Pedro J Copado-Mendez, P.: Resolution of coupling order and station level constraints in train unit scheduling. Public Transp. **14**, 27–61 (2022). https://doi.org/10.1007/s12469-022-00295-3
29. Lin, Z., Kwan, R.S.K.: An integer fixed-charge multicommodity flow (FCMF) model for train unit scheduling. Electron. Notes Discrete Math. **41**, 165–172 (2013)
30. Lin, Z., Barrena, E., Kwan, R.S.K.: Train unit scheduling guided by historic capacity provisions and passenger count surveys. Public Transp. **9**(1-2), 137–154 (2017)
31. Lin, Z., Kwan, R.S.K.: A two-phase approach for real-world train unit scheduling. Public Transp. **6**(1), 35–65 (2014)
32. Lin, Z., Kwan, R.S.K.: Local convex hulls for a special class of integer multicommodity flow problems. Comput. Optim. Appl. **64**(3), 881–919 (2016). https://doi.org/10.1007/s10589-016-9831-3
33. Lin, Z., Kwan, R.S.: A branch-and-price approach for solving the train unit scheduling problem. Transp. Res. Part B Methodol. **94**, 97–120 (2016)

34. Lloyd, S.: Least squares quantization in PCM. IEEE Trans. Inf. Theor. **28**(2), 129–137 (1982)
35. Macqueen, J.: Some methods for classification and analysis of multivariate observations. In: In 5-th Berkeley Symposium on Mathematical Statistics and Probability, pp. 281–297 (1967)
36. Maróti, G., Gerards, A.M.H., Kroon, L.G., Eindhoven, T.: Operations research models for railway rolling stock planning (2006)
37. Peeters, M., Kroon, L.: Circulation of railway rolling stock: a branch-and-price approach. Comput. & OR. **35**, 538–556 (2008)
38. Preud'homme, G., et al.: Head-to-head comparison of clustering methods for heterogeneous data: a simulation-driven benchmark. Sci. Rep. **11**(1), 1–14 (2021)
39. Schrijver, A.: Minimum circulation of railway stock. CWI Q. **6**, 205–217 (1993)
40. Srikanth, K., Reddy, S.R., Swathi, T.: A novel supervised machine learning algorithm for intrusion detection: K-prototype+id3. Int. J. Eng. Res. Technol. **3**, 1475–1480 (2014)
41. Talbi, E.G.: A taxonomy of hybrid metaheuristics. J. Heuristics **8**, 541–564 (2002)

ACC Fuzzy-Based Control Architecture for Multi-body High-Speed Trains with Active Inter-cars Couplers

Giacomo Basile$^{(\boxtimes)}$ ⓘ, Dario Giuseppe Lui ⓘ, Alberto Petrillo ⓘ, and Stefania Santini ⓘ

DIETI, Università Degli Studi di Napoli Federico II, Via Claudio 21,
80125 Naples, Italy
{giacomo.basile,dariogiuseppe.lui,alberto.petrillo,
stefania.santini}@unina.it

Abstract. This paper tackles the problem of controlling the motion of high-speed train composed of different cars physically connected via active couplers, where only the first one is powered. At high-speed, performing acceleration and deceleration maneuvers could generate higher longitudinal inter-cars coupling forces, which might cause possible shocks of the couplers compromising their mechanical structure and, hence, the safety during the travel. To face this issue, we propose a novel double layer control architecture able to guarantee that the whole high-speed train moves according to an Adaptive Cruise Control (ACC) guidance mode, while reducing inter-cars shocking phenomena. Accordingly, we design a PID controller for driving the motion of the first powered car and a Fuzzy-based PI for the active couplers. More in details, the fuzzy logic is used to modulate the damping and spring coefficients of each active coupler with the aim of reducing the higher fluctuations of the coupling force induced by couplers for travelling, hence minimizing the inter-cars shocks. Numerical results, including a comparison analysis with a passive coupler, confirm the effectiveness and the benefits of the proposed control architecture in guaranteeing a smooth and safe inter-cars motion.

Keywords: High-speed trains · Multi-body trains dynamics · Inter-cars shocking phenomena · Adaptive Cruise Control · Fuzzy control

1 Introduction

In the last years, the railway systems have been technologically improved with the introduction of novel infrastructures and high-speed trains model [12]. More in detail, trains have been updated to run at higher speed and with a more loading capacity. In this scenario, the speed tracking control is a fundamental requirement for the punctuality of the operation of a train, which leads to an increase in the automatic train operation control capabilities of high-speed trains [20].

S. Marrone et al. (Eds.): EDCC 2022 Workshops, CCIS 1656, pp. 126–138, 2022.
https://doi.org/10.1007/978-3-031-16245-9_10

Specifically, great efforts have been devoted to the speed control design for high-speed trains, such as active communication-based control [5,24], iterative learning control [4,26], adaptive control [10], and so on.

In the above mentioned literature, the high-speed train is mainly modelled via the single mass point model where intra-train dynamics among the different rail cars is neglected.

However, another possible way of modelling the behaviour of a high speed train is due to the multi-body model, i.e. a cascade of mass points physically connected via mechanical coupler [6,13]. While the single mass point model is exploited for designing speed tracking control strategy, the multi-body one allows considering the inter-connection dynamics among cars which are crucial at high-speed, especially when performing acceleration and deceleration maneuvers [11]. Indeed, for ensuring that the whole train could track a desired imposed reference behaviour, without compromising the mechanical structure of the couplers and, hence the travel safety, it is necessary to contain the fluctuations of the coupling forces [8].

Within this context, the problem is addressed by considering both, passive and active couplers. The former, including the bump stop, damper, friction, pin link and shear spring, air spring and bush, are characterized by a proper nonlinear fixed stiffness characteristics [17]. The latter, instead, exploits active elements, for example, magnetorheological dampers [2], whose characteristics can be properly controlled on the basis of the encountered operative conditions [15].

By exploiting passive dampers, [18] proposes a distributed and fault-tolerant control design approach to develop tracking and braking control schemes while [22] suggests a tracking controller for high-speed trains leveraging multi-agent technology. Again, in [19], by using multi-particle model, a robust control criterion for the velocity tracking control of high-speed trains is developed. By assuming, instead, which some of the cars belonging to the high speed trains are powered, [11] suggests an adaptive Lyapunov-based controllers.

Conversely, by exploiting active controllable couplers, [16] proposes a control architecture aiming to reduce the coupling force via a robust model-based control for magnetorheological dampers. Again, by leveraging a proper model of the active couplers, [8] suggests a PID-based control architecture to adapt the stiffness characteristic of the inter-cars junctions.

Nevertheless, the aforementioned control strategies require the knowledge of couplers model and this make the proposed solution properly tailored for the specific appraised case of study.

To face this issue, in this work we propose a double layer control architecture composed of: i) a PID controller for driving the motion of the whole train and acting only on the first powered car; ii) a fuzzy-based gain scheduling PI control able to adapt the stiffness properties of the active couplers, for reducing inter-cars shocks phenomena, without requiring the knowledge of its dynamical model but only the maximum allowable coupling force they can induce.

Numerical analysis, also including a comparison analysis w.r.t. the performance achievable via a passive couplers, corroborate the effectiveness of the proposed control architecture in guaranteeing the motion control of high-speed trains with a reduction of the inter-cars coupling forces fluctuations.

Finally, the paper is organized as follows: Sect. 2 presents the force analysis of the rail cars model, the overall Multi-body high-speed train model and the control requirements. In Sect. 3 we propose the control architecture and we provide details about the designed Adaptive Cruise Control (ACC) controller and the Fuzzy-Pi controller 3.2. Numerical validation, including comparison analysis with the performance achievable with passive couplers is presented in Subsect. 4. Finally, conclusions are drawn in Sect. 5.

2   System Description and Problem Statement

Consider a high-speed train composed by $N+1$ heterogeneous rail cars, physically connected via N full-automatic couplers, where the first car, indexed with 0 is the powered one.

In our operative scenario, each car is equipped with leaky coaxial synthesized optical cable and the fiber optic gyroscope inertial navigation system, able to accurately measure its position and speed [3,25]. Our aim is to properly control the coupling force of each physical coupler j $(j = 1, \cdots, N)$ connecting consecutive cars $(i; i - 1)$ $(i = 0, 1, \cdots, N)$ so to guarantee safety during the travel, hence reducing shocks on endurance of the weakest train structural components.

2.1   Multi-body High-Speed Train Dynamics

The behaviour of each rail car i is modeled as point mass system. Specifically, its motion is described by the longitudinal dynamics which, including the driving/braking propulsion system, the aerodynamic drag and the inter-cars coupling forces, are described via the following nonlinear system [6,13]:

$$
\begin{aligned}
\dot{p}_i(t) &= v_i(t) \\
M_i \dot{v}_i(t) &= u_i(t) - M_i\, R_i(v_i(t)) + F_{c,i-1,i}(t) \\
&\quad - F_{c,i,i+1}(t) - F_{\mu,i}(t) - \omega_i(t),
\end{aligned}
\tag{1}
$$

where $p_i(t)$ [m], $v_i(t)$ [m/s] are the position and speed of i-th car, respectively; $u_i(t)$ [kg m/s^2] is the control input representing the longitudinal acceleration to be imposed by the control system; M_i [kg] is the i-th car mass; $R_i(v_i(t)) = \mathrm{sign}(v_i(t))(C_{1,i} + C_{2,i}\,|v_i(t)| + C_{3,i}\,v_i(t)^2)$ is the propulsion resistance expressed via the Davis formula [7]; $C_{3,i}$, $C_{2,i}$, $C_{1,i}$ represent the Davis parameters of the aerodynamic drag; $\omega_i(t)$ [m/s^2] is the external disturbance force acting on the train dynamics; $F_{\mu,i} = \mu\, M_i\, g\, sin(\theta)$ is the friction force where μ is the friction constant steal-steal while θ is the track slope; $F_{c,i-1,i}(t)$ and $F_{c,i,i+1}(t)$ are the coupling forces, due to active couplers, modelled as:

$$
\begin{aligned}
F_{c,i,i-1}(t) =& k_j(u^*_{f,j})\,(p_{i-1}(t) - p_i(t)) \\
&+ b_j(u^*_{f,j})\,(v_{i-1}(t) - v_i(t)), && \forall i = 1, \cdots, N \\
F_{c,i,i+1}(t) =& k_{j+1}(u^*_{f,j+1})\,(p_i(t) - p_{i+1}(t)) \\
&+ b_{j+1}(u^*_{f,j+1})\,(v_i(t) - v_{i+1}(t)), && \forall i = 0, \cdots, N-1
\end{aligned}
\tag{2}
$$

where k_j, k_{j+1} and b_j, b_{j+1} are the spring and damping coefficients for the j-th and $j+1$-th couplers (being $j = i$), respectively.

Note that the damping coefficients vary based on the desired control inputs $u^*_{f,j}$ and $u^*_{f,j+1}$ to be imposed on the j-th and $j+1$-th full-automatic couplers, respectively, to avoid coupling shocks.

Based on the force analysis, the multi-body high speed train composed of $N + 1$ cars physically connected via N couplers can be described by following differential dynamical system:

$$
\begin{aligned}
\dot{p}_0(t) =& v_0(t) \\
M_0 \dot{v}_0(t) =& u_0(t) - F_{c,0,1}(t) - F_{\mu,0} - \omega_0(t) \\
& - (C_{1,0} + C_{2,0}\,\|v_0(t)\| + C_{3,0}\,v_0(t)^2)
\end{aligned}
\tag{3}
$$

$$
\begin{aligned}
\dot{p}_1(t) =& v_1(t) \\
M_1 \dot{v}_1(t) =& F_{c,1,0}(t) - F_{c,1,2}(t) - F_{\mu,1}
\end{aligned}
\tag{4}
$$

$$
\vdots
$$

$$
\begin{aligned}
\dot{p}_i(t) =& v_i(t) \\
M_i \dot{v}_i(t) =& F_{c,i,i-1}(t) - F_{c,i,i+1}(t) - F_{\mu,i}
\end{aligned}
\tag{5}
$$

$$
\vdots
$$

$$
\begin{aligned}
\dot{p}_N(t) =& v_N(t) \\
M_N \dot{v}_N(t) =& F_{c,N,N-1}(t) - F_{\mu,N}
\end{aligned}
\tag{6}
$$

Note that according to the physical constraints, the air-drag force and external disturbances act only on the first powered car [11].

2.2 Control Objective

The control objective is to guarantee that the high-speed train moves according to an Adaptive Cruise Control (ACC) mode while adapting, at the same time, the force required by each coupler j ($j = 1, \cdots, N$) so to reduce shocks during the overall train motion by minimizing the fluctuations of the coupling forces.

Therefore, the control problem consists in designing a control architecture able to fulfill the following requirements: i) computing a speed profile to be imposed on the multi-body trains dynamics according to ACC mode, i.e. find $u_0(t)$ in (3) such that

$$
\begin{aligned}
\lim_{t \to +\infty} \|v_c(t) - v_0(t)\| = 0, \\
\lim_{t \to +\infty} \|p_c(t) - p_0(t) - d_{c0}\| = 0
\end{aligned}
\tag{7}
$$

being $v_c(t)$ and $p_c(t)$ the reference time-varying travelling profile to be tracked (being d_{c0} the desired distance at standstill w.r.t. the reference position), despite the presence of external disturbances acting on the vehicle dynamics; ii) ensuring that all cars move according to the ACC mode while avoiding strong shocks on the couplers, hence preserving the mechanical structure and the correct functioning of the junctions, i.e. find $u_{f,j}^*$ ($\forall j$) related to the consecutive cars couple $(i, i-1)$ in (4)–(5)–(6) and adapt the damping and spring coefficient, i.e. $b_j(u_{f,j}^*)$ and $k_j(u_{f,j}^*)$, in order to minimize fluctuations of the coupling force (2).

3   ACC Fuzzy-Based Control Architecture

To solve the problem stated in Sect. 2.2, we propose the double-layer control architecture depicted in Fig. 1.

It is composed of: i) a PID control driving the overall train motion and acting on the power car according to the ACC guidance mode; ii) a Fuzzy PI controller which acts on each coupler j ($j = 1, \cdots, N$) by adapting its damping and spring coefficient so to generate a coupling force able to reduce shocking inter-cars dangerous phenomena.

3.1   ACC Control Strategy

In this section, we design the control action $u_0(t)$ able to satisfy the first control aim (7) as the following PID strategy

$$u_i(t) = k_p\, e_p(t) + k_i \int_0^t e_p(t)\, dt + k_d\, e_v(t), \tag{8}$$

where $e_p(t) = p_c(t) - p_0(t) - d_{c0}$ and $e_v(t) = v_c(t) - v_0(t)$; k_p, k_i and k_d are the proportional, integral and derivative gains to be properly tuned.

They are tuned according to the Lyapunov-based tuning rule proposed in [9] as: $k_p = 40$, $k_i = 1.5$, $k_d = 0.1$.

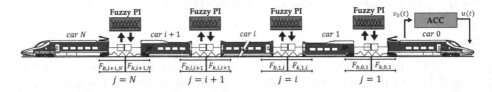

Fig. 1. Overview of the proposed double layer ACC fuzzy-based control architecture for multi-body high-speed trains.

3.2   Anti-fluctuation Fuzzy-Based PI Controller

To achieve the control aim ii stated in Sect. 2.2 we propose a fuzzy-based gain scheduling PI controller which acts in a twofold way as shown in Fig. 2. Firstly, the strategy computes the desired coupling force $u_{f,j}^*$ able to avoid strong inter-car shocks, hence minimizing the inter-cars fluctuations.

Then, based on this value, the protocol properly imposes the value of the damping and spring coefficient for the coupler in order to realize the desired coupling force $u^*_{f,j}$.

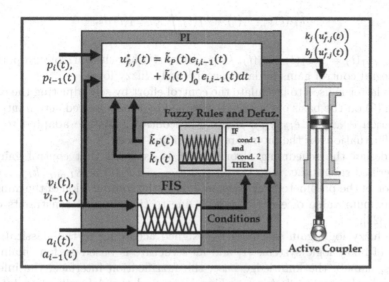

Fig. 2. Overview of the fuzzy-based PI controller and how it acts on the active coupler.

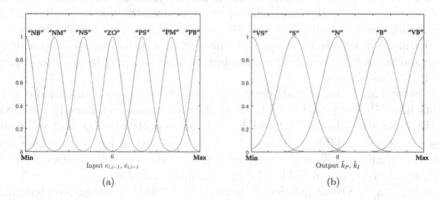

(a)   (b)

Fig. 3. Membership function for: a) the input variables $e_{i,i-1}(t)$ and $\dot{e}_{i,i-1}(t)$; b) the output variables $\tilde{k}_P$ and $\tilde{k}_I$

The desired coupling force is computed $\forall j$ according to a PI structure with variable gains as

$$
\begin{aligned}
u^*_{f,j}(t) =& \tilde{k}_P(t)\,(v_{i-1}(t) - v_i(t)) + \tilde{k}_I(t)(p_{i-1}(t) - p_i(t)), \\
=& \tilde{k}_P(t)\,e_{i,i-1}(t) + \tilde{k}_I(t)\int_0^t e_{i,i-1}(t)\,dt,
\end{aligned}
\tag{9}
$$

where $e_{i,i-1}(t) = v_{i-1}(t) - v_i(t)$; $\tilde{k}_P(t)$ and $\tilde{k}_I(t)$ are the variable proportional and integral control gains updated according to fuzzy logic.

This latter is used to modulate the control effort by self adjusting the control gains in (9) on the basis of the values assumed by the measured actual inter-cars information $e_{i,i-1}(t)$, $\dot{e}_{i,i-1}(t)$. Hence, the control gains are adapted to avoid strong fluctuations of the inter-cars position and speed.

To design the scheduling algorithm, it is assumed that control gains are in prescribed ranges, i.e., $\tilde{k}_P(t) = [k_{P,min}, k_{P,max}]$; $\tilde{k}_I(t) = [k_{I,min}, k_{I,max}]$. The definition of the parameters regions and, hence, the computation of the minimum and maximum value of each PI gain is due to the physical constraints of the coupler [23].

The fuzzy logic gain scheduler is designed according to the classical architecture of fuzzy logic systems [1] and its structure is based on four main components, namely the knowledge base, the fuzzification interface, the inference engine, also known as decision making logic, and the defuzzification interface [1]. The knowledge base system contains all the information required for the fuzzy system, namely the fuzzy control rule base and the data base. The inference engine performs inference procedures upon the fuzzy control rules, while the fuzzification interface defines a mapping from a real-value space to a fuzzy space and the defuzzification interface implements a mapping from a fuzzy space to a real-valued space.

In what follows we provide details on each of the components for our two-inputs fuzzy PI configuration. The exemplary Gaussian membership functions for the input variable $e_{i,i-1}(t)$ and $\dot{e}_{i,i-1}(t)$ are reported in Fig. 3(a) while the ones for output variable $\tilde{k}_P(t)$ and $\tilde{k}_I(t)$ are depicted in Fig. 3(b), whose features (i.e. minimum/maximum value, the mean and standard deviation for each function) are reported in Table 1 for each involved variable.

In Fig. 3(a), "NB" stands for "Negative Big", "NM" is "Negative Medium", "NS" is "Negative Small", "Zero" is "ZO", "PS" represents "Positive Small", and "PM" and "PB" stand for "Positive Medium" and "Positive Big". Conversely, the membership function for the fuzzy outputs, shown in Fig. 3(b) define five inference regions, where "VS" stands for "Very Small", "S" for "Small", "N" is "Normal", "B" is "Big", "VB" represents "Very Big". The knowledge base, reported in Table 2 is built according to [14].

Table 1. Membership function rules parameters set

Parameter	value	Parameter	value
$e_{i,i-1}\,min$	$-2.5\,[kN]$	μ_e	$[-2.5, -1.25, -0.75, 0.0, 0.75, 1.25, 2.5]\,[kN]$
$e_{i,i-1}\,max$	$2.5\,[kN]$	σ_e	$0.45[kN]$
$\dot{e}_{i,i-1}\,min$	$-0.8\,[kN]$	$\mu_{\tilde{k}_p}$	$[-1.8, -0.9, 0, 0.9, 1.8] \times 10^5\,[kN]$
$\dot{e}_{i,i-1}\,max$	$0.8\,[kN]$	$\sigma_{\tilde{k}_p}$	$0.08\,[kN]$
$\tilde{k}_P\,min$	$-1.8 \times 10^5\,[kN]$	$\mu_{\dot{e}}$	$[-0.8, -0.58, -0.26, 0.0, 0.58, 0.26, 0.8]\,[kN]$
$\tilde{k}_P\,max$	$1,8 \times 10^5\,[kN]$	$\sigma_{\dot{e}}$	$0.45 \times 10^4\,[kN]$
$\tilde{k}_I\,min$	$-5.1 \times 10^5\,[kN]$	$\mu_{\tilde{k}_i}$	$[-5.1, -2.5, 0, 2.5, 5.1] \times 10^5\,[kN]$
$\tilde{k}_I\,max$	$5.1 \times 10^5\,[kN]$	$\sigma_{\tilde{k}_i}$	$0.45 \times 10^4\,[kN]$

Table 2. Fuzzy tuning rules

(a) Fuzzy rules tuning for $\tilde{k}_P(t) \rightarrow K$

		$e_{i,i-1}(t)$						
		NB	NM	NS	ZO	PS	PM	PB
$\dot{e}_{i,i-1}(t)$	NB	B	B	B	B	B	B	B
	NM	S	B	B	B	B	B	S
	NS	S	S	B	B	B	S	S
	ZO	S	S	S	B	S	S	S
	PS	S	S	B	B	B	S	S
	PM	S	B	B	B	B	B	S
	PB	B	B	B	B	B	B	B

(b) Fuzzy rules tuning for $\tilde{k}_I(t) \rightarrow I$

		$e_{i,i-1}(t)$						
		NB	NM	NS	ZO	PS	PM	PB
$\dot{e}_{i,i-1}(t)$	NB	VS	VS	VS	VS	VS	VS	VS
	NM	S	S	VS	VS	VS	S	S
	NS	B	S	S	VS	S	S	B
	ZO	VB	B	S	VS	VS	B	VB
	PS	B	S	S	VS	S	S	B
	PM	S	S	VS	VS	VS	S	S
	PB	VS	VS	VS	VS	VS	VS	VS

Specifically, Table 2(a) defines the relationship between the two input membership function (i.e. $e_{i,i-1}(t)$ and $\dot{e}_{i,i-1}(t)$) and the membership function of $\tilde{k}_P(t)$ while Table 2(b) determines the relationship between the two input membership function and the membership function of $\tilde{k}_I(t)$. Considering the above defined knowledge base, we construct 49 fuzzy rules for each control gains to be tuned.

Note that, the selection of fuzzy rules is one of the important aspects to be considered to achieve smoother response and less oscillation at the transient state. To this aim, fuzzy rules are selected similar to [14] and they are of the form

$$\textbf{if } e_{i,i-1}(t) \in A_n \wedge \dot{e}_{i,i-1}(t) \in B_m \textbf{ then}$$
$$k_P(t) = K;$$
$$k_I(t) = I;$$

$$\textbf{end}$$

where A_n and B_m are the region sets defined by the input membership function $e_{i,i-1}(t)$ and $\dot{e}_{i,i-1}(t)$ respectively, while K and I are the proper value of the control gains related to the active output inference regions.

These latter values are defuzzified via the Center of Gravity method (COG) method [21], hence obtaining the control gain value $\tilde{k}_P$ and $\tilde{k}_I$ able to guarantee the minimization of the coupling force fluctuations. Finally the proper value of the j-th coupler spring and damping are set as:

$$k_j(u_{f,j}^*) = \tilde{k}_I(t)$$
$$b_j(u_{f,j}^*) = \tilde{k}_P(t). \tag{10}$$

4   Numerical Results

In this section, we test the effectiveness of the proposed ACC Fuzzy-based control architecture presented in Sect. 3 for a multi-body high-speed train composed of $N = 3$ cars physically connected via 2 active couplers. Train dynamics parameters are reported in Table 3 [11].

The external disturbances acting on the dynamics of the powered car is modelled as $w_0(t) = 0.3\,sin(0.5\,t)$ while the track slope is emulated, according to the typical Italian railways, as a time-varying function within the range $[0°, 5°]$.

As driving scenario, we consider an exemplary trapezoidal maneuver, where the desired reference speed $v_c(t)$ is chosen such that, starting from an initial speed of 55.0 [m/s], the first car has to accelerate, at $t = 20$ [s], until reaching the speed of 73 [m/s] at $t = 35$ [s]. Then, at 65 [s], a braking maneuver is required until reaching the constant speed of 55 [m/s]. Regarding the initial reference position, it is set as $p_c = 1000$ [m] while the desired distance at standstill is chosen as $d_{c0} = 100$ [m].

During the whole maneuver, the Fuzzy PI, acting on each fully-automatic coupler j ($j = 1, 2$), set the proper values of the damping and spring so to minimize the fluctuations of the coupling forces.

Table 3. Multi-body high-speed train parameters

Parameter	Value
M_1	35 [ton]
M_2	35 [ton]
M_3	35 [ton]
$C_{3,0}$	6.63 [1/m]
$C_{2,0}$	5.43 [1/s]
$C_{1,0}$	0.001 [m/s^2]
μ_i $(i = 1, 2, 3)$	0.001 [−]
a_{max}	1.2 [m/s^2]
a_{min}	−1.2 [m/s^2]

Results in Fig. 4 and Fig. 5 disclose the ability of the proposed control architecture in guaranteeing that the multi-body high-speed train moves according to the ACC mode while guaranteeing the boundedness of the coupling forces, hence preserving the mechanical structure and correct functioning of couplers, despite the presence of external disturbances. Indeed each car tracks the reference speed profile (see Fig. 4(a)) with very small bounded inter-cars position and speed errors (see Fig. 4(b)–(c) respectively).

This latter behaviour is due to coupling force generated by each coupler j $(j = 1, 2)$ (see Fig. 5(a)) which present a smooth behaviour thanks to the adaptation of the control gains $k_j(t)$ (see Fig. 5(b)) and $b_j(t)$ (see Fig. 5(c)).

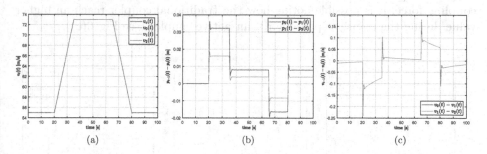

(a)   (b)   (c)

Fig. 4. Performance of the ACC fuzzy-based control architecture. Time history of: (a) cars speed profile $v_i(t)$ $(i = 0, 1, 2)$ plus the reference behaviour $v_c(t)$; (b) position errors $e_{i-1,i}(t) = p_{i-1}(t) - p_i(t)$ $(i = 1, 2)$; (c) speed errors $\dot{e}_{i-1,i}(t) = v_{i-1}(t) - v_i(t)$ $(i = 1, 2)$.

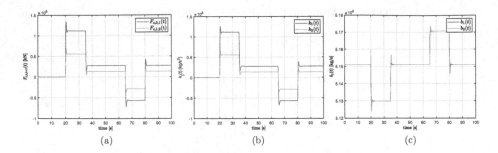

(a)   (b)   (c)

Fig. 5. Performance of the ACC fuzzy-based control architecture. Time history of: (a) inter-cars coupling force $F_{c,i,i+1}(t)$ $(i = 0, 1)$; (b) spring coefficient trends $k_j(u_{f,j}^*)$ $(j = 1, 2)$ computed by the Fuzzy-PI controller; (c) dumping coefficient trends $b_j(u_{f,j}^*)$ $(j = 1, 2)$ computed by the Fuzzy-PI controller.

4.1   Comparison Analysis

Now, to better appreciate the benefits of the proposed control Fuzzy PI strategy, we compare its performance with the one achievable with the passive couplers usually presented on the traditional train as metro, freight trains and high speed trains. Specifically, the coupler are characterized with a spring and damping fixed to $k_j = 50 \times 10^5$ [kg/s²] and $b_j = 2 \times 10^4$ [kg/s] $(j = 1, 2)$ [11].

Comparison results are depicted in Fig. 6. Herein it is possible to appreciate the benefits of the proposed controller w.r.t. passive coupler. Indeed the position and speed errors due to the passive coupler present a non-smooth behaviour with significant oscillations (see Fig. 6(a)–(b)) while a better performances are achieved by the proposed Fuzzy-PI controller (see Fig. 4(b)–(c)). Regarding the coupling force, it is possible noting how the traditional coupler reach an higher value during the transient phase w.r.t. an active coupler (see Fig. 6(c)).

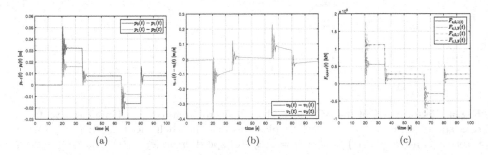

(a)   (b)   (c)

Fig. 6. Comparison analysis between the proposed ACC fuzzy-based control architecture and a passive coupler with fixed spring and damping. Time history of: (a) position errors $e_{i-1,i}(t) = p_{i-1}(t) - p_i(t)$ $(i = 1, 2)$ guaranteed by the passive coupler; (b) speed errors $\dot{e}_{i-1,i}(t) = v_{i-1}(t) - v_i(t)$ $(i = 1, 2)$ guaranteed by the passive coupler; (c) comparison between the coupling force $F_{c,i,i+1}(t)$ $(i = 0, 1)$ ensured by the proposed ACC fuzzy-based control architecture (i.e. continuous line) and the ones ensured by the passive coupler (i.e. dashed lines).

5 Conclusions

This paper have addressed the problem of controlling the motion of multi-body high-speed trains composed of $N+1$ cars physically connected through active couplers, where only the first one is powered. To solve the problem a double layer ACC Fuzzy-based control architecture, able to drive their longitudinal dynamics while ensuring the reduction of inter-cars shocks phenomena, has been proposed. In details, a PID controller has been designed for imposing to the first powered car the ACC guidance mode while a Fuzzy PI has been suggested for adapting the spring and damping coefficients of the active couplers so to reduce the fluctuations induced by inter-cars coupling forces. Numerical simulations has disclosed the effectiveness and the advantages of the proposed control architecture.

References

1. Babuška, R.: Fuzzy Modeling for Control, vol. 12. Springer Science & Business Media, New York (2012)
2. Brancati, R., Di Massa, G., Pagano, S., Petrillo, A., Santini, S.: A combined neural network and model predictive control approach for ball transfer unit-magnetorheological elastomer-based vibration isolation of lightweight structures. J. Vibr. Control **26**(19–20), 1668–1682 (2020)
3. Chou, M., Xia, X., Kayser, C.: Modelling and model validation of heavy-haul trains equipped with electronically controlled pneumatic brake systems. Control Eng. Pract. **15**(4), 501–509 (2007)
4. Di Meo, C., Di Vaio, M., Flammini, F., Nardone, R., Santini, S., Vittorini, V.: ERTMS/ETCS virtual coupling: proof of concept and numerical analysis. IEEE Trans. Intell. Transp. Syst. **21**(6), 2545–2556 (2019)
5. Flammini, F., Marrone, S., Nardone, R., Petrillo, A., Santini, S., Vittorini, V.: Towards railway virtual coupling. In: 2018 IEEE International Conference on Electrical Systems for Aircraft, Railway, Ship Propulsion and Road Vehicles & International Transportation Electrification Conference (ESARS-ITEC), pp. 1–6. IEEE (2018)
6. Garg, V.: Dynamics of Railway Vehicle Systems. Elsevier, Amsterdam (2012)
7. Iwnicki, S.: Handbook of Railway Vehicle Dynamics. CRC Press, Boca Raton (2006)
8. Jackiewicz, J.: Coupler force reduction method for multiple-unit trains using a new hierarchical control system. Railway Eng. Sci. **29**(2), 163–182 (2021). https://doi.org/10.1007/s40534-021-00239-w
9. Manfredi, S., Petrillo, A., Santini, S.: Distributed pi control for heterogeneous nonlinear platoon of autonomous connected vehicles. IFAC-PapersOnLine **53**(2), 15229–15234 (2020)
10. Mao, Z., Tao, G., Jiang, B., Yan, X.G.: Adaptive compensation of traction system actuator failures for high-speed trains. IEEE Trans. Intell. Transp. Syst. **18**(11), 2950–2963 (2017)
11. Mao, Z., Tao, G., Jiang, B., Yan, X.G.: Adaptive control design and evaluation for multibody high-speed train dynamic models. IEEE Trans. Control Syst. Technol. **29**(3), 1061–1074 (2021). https://doi.org/10.1109/TCST.2020.2991119

12. Niu, Y., Zhao, X., Wang, Y., Deng, X.: Locomotive model for international competitive advantages paths of high-speed railway contractors. J. Infrastruct. Syst. **27**(2), 04021002 (2021)
13. Park, J., Lee, B.H., Eun, Y.: Virtual coupling of railway vehicles: gap reference for merge and separation, robust control, and position measurement. IEEE Trans. Intell. Transp. Syst. **23**(2), 1085–1096 (2020)
14. Persico, V., Grimaldi, D., Pescape, A., Salvi, A., Santini, S.: A fuzzy approach based on heterogeneous metrics for scaling out public clouds. IEEE Trans. Parallel Distrib. Syst. **28**(8), 2117–2130 (2017)
15. Sharma, S.K., Kumar, A.: Ride performance of a high speed rail vehicle using controlled semi active suspension system. Smart Mater. Struct. **26**(5), 055026 (2017)
16. Sharma, S.K., Saini, U., Kumar, A.: Semi-active control to reduce lateral vibration of passenger rail vehicle using disturbance rejection and continuous state damper controllers. J. Vib. Eng. Technol. **7**(2), 117–129 (2019). https://doi.org/10.1007/s42417-019-00088-2
17. Sharma, S.K., Sharma, R.C., Kumar, A., Palli, S.: Challenges in rail vehicle-track modeling and simulation. Int. J. Veh. Struct. Syst. **7**(1), 1–9 (2015)
18. Song, Q., Song, Y.D., Tang, T., Ning, B.: Computationally inexpensive tracking control of high-speed trains with traction/braking saturation. IEEE Trans. Intell. Transp. Syst. **12**(4), 1116–1125 (2011)
19. Tang, H., Wang, Q., Feng, X.: Robust stochastic control for high-speed trains with nonlinearity, parametric uncertainty, and multiple time-varying delays. IEEE Trans. Intell. Transp. Syst. **19**(4), 1027–1037 (2017)
20. Tasiu, I.A., Liu, Z., Wu, S., Yu, W., Al-Barashi, M., Ojo, J.O.: Review of recent control strategies for the traction converters in high-speed train. IEEE Trans. Transp. Electrification **8**(2), 2311–2333 (2022)
21. Van Leekwijck, W., Kerre, E.E.: Defuzzification: criteria and classification. Fuzzy Sets Syst. **108**(2), 159–178 (1999)
22. Wang, Y., Song, Y., Gao, H., Lewis, F.L.: Distributed fault-tolerant control of virtually and physically interconnected systems with application to high-speed trains under traction/braking failures. IEEE Trans. Intell. Transp. Syst. **17**(2), 535–545 (2016). https://doi.org/10.1109/TITS.2015.2479922
23. Zeng, X., Zhang, L., Yu, Y., Shi, M., Zhou, J.: The stiffness and damping characteristics of a dual-chamber air spring device applied to motion suppression of marine structures. Appl. Sci. **6**(3), 74 (2016)
24. Zhang, L., Zhou, M., Li, Z., et al.: An intelligent train operation method based on event-driven deep reinforcement learning. IEEE Trans. Ind. Inform. **18**(10), 6973–6980 (2021)
25. Zhang, S., Zhang, W., Jin, X.: Dynamics of high speed wheel/rail system and its modelling. Chin. Sci. Bull. **52**(11), 1566–1575 (2007). https://doi.org/10.1007/s11434-007-0213-1
26. Zhou, X., Wang, H., Tian, Y., Dai, X.: Consensus tracking via quantized iterative learning control for singular nonlinear multi-agent systems with state time-delay and initial state error. Nonlinear Dyn. **103**(3), 2701–2719 (2021). https://doi.org/10.1007/s11071-021-06265-x

Onboard Sensor Systems for Automatic Train Operation

Rustam Tagiew[1]($\boxtimes$) (iD), Dirk Leinhos[2], Henrik von der Haar[2],
Christian Klotz[1](iD), Dennis Sprute[3](iD), Jens Ziehn[3](iD), Andreas Schmelter[4],
Stefan Witte[4], and Pavel Klasek[2](iD)

[1] German Centre for Rail Traffic Research at Federal Railway Authority,
Dresden, Germany
{tagiewr,klotzc,klasekp}@dzsf.bund.de
[2] DB Systemtechnik GmbH, Minden, Germany
{dirk.leinhos,henrik.von-der-haar}@deutschebahn.de
[3] Fraunhofer IOSB, Karlsruhe, Germany
{dennis.sprute,jens.ziehn}@iosbfraunhofer.de
[4] Technische Hochschule OWL, Lemgo, Germany
{andreas.schmelter,stefan.witte}@th-owl.de

Abstract. This paper introduces the specific requirements of the
domain of train operation and its regulatory framework to the AI community. It assesses sensor sets for driverless and unattended train operation.
It lists functionally justified ranges of technical specifications for sensors
of different types, which will generate input for AI perception algorithms
(i.e. for signal and obstacle detection). Since an optimal sensor set is the
subject of research, this paper provides the specification of a generic
data acquisition platform as a crucial step. Some particular results are
recommendations for the minimal resolution and shutter type for image
sensors, as well as beam steering methods and resolutions for LiDARs.

Keywords: Automatic train operation · ATO · GoA3 · GoA4 ·
Perception · AI

1 Introduction

Automated driving is of great importance for the rail sector to achieve the goals
of raising the capacity and the modal share for both passenger and freight traffic in Europe. The advantages and potentials of the introduction of automatic
train operation (ATO) in rail transport in Germany are well known [5]. Technical possibilities for the realization of higher Grades of Automation (GoA) in
future rail systems are currently being researched and implemented as examples
in various projects [12]. In particular, driverless train operation under GoA3 and
unattended train operation under GoA4 summarized as GoA3+, pose various

Supported by German Centre for Rail Traffic Research DISCLAIMER: This is not an
official statement, guideline or directive of the German Federal Railway Authority.

challenges [29]. In GoA3+, the responsibilities of the human driver are handed over to a technical system. This includes a variety of tasks where the drivers' abilities of perception, recognition and reasoning are involved. The implementation of the first two of these functions will most probably not be possible without using AI algorithms in many operational scenarios [26]. AI development in turn is data-driven. The algorithms require large amounts of data for training, validation and testing. To issue approval for a driverless vehicle, the functional safety of the technical system has to be analyzed and risk mitigation must be proven. It is, therefore, necessary to identify all the system functions and respective tasks for the driver or the perception system and to prove the ability of the system to solve these tasks reliably.

In the automotive industry, automated driving is also under development. The manufacturers are cooperating. Open vision data sets of sensor data, collected in real traffic situations, are available and used in the R&D community. In [30], at least 60 vision data sets available for automotive application have been identified (well-known examples include the KITTI Vision Benchmark Suite [15], Cityscapes [8] or BDD100K [33]), while for the rail sector only two data sets were available [16, 34]. This and other reviews [25, e.g.] emphasize the need for the railway sector to produce and share open data sets of similar breadth and quality for the future development. To achieve this, a set of sensors has to be defined for the data collection. By now it is not possible to assess exactly the sensor setup needed for GoA3+ implementation since further research is necessary to develop and prove the systems. Hence, a sensor setup for R&D purposes has to be defined first with a slightly different scope compared to a productive setup.

Since data needed for AI development is only conditionally compatible among different sensor sets, a scientific study of sensor set variations and suitability for the rail domain becomes necessary for the advancement of the aforementioned technology. Such a scientific study was carried out in the departmental research project "ATO Sensorik" for the German Centre for Rail Traffic Research [22]. One of the main results of this study was a requirement analysis for the technical system, which is an important piece of knowledge for the community of AI researchers. This requirement analysis is based on investigation of legitimate tasks of a train driver. The results contribute to a common understanding within the community on state-of-art technical implementations in the light of a regulatory framework on the case example of Germany. A unanimously agreed solution for a sensor setup is in discussion and does not exist yet.

In this paper, we will start with a brief overview of the key results of the requirement analysis in Sect. 2. Subsequently, Sect. 3 presents how future AI applications introduce requirements for the diversity of the sensor setup foster research on domain gaps and their mitigation. Section 4 outlines the sensor setup that was specified to satisfy the perception requirements with the diversity required according to Sect. 2. Sect. 5 draws the main conclusions from the results and provide an outlook of required steps towards the provision of large scale and high quality open data sets for rail applications that meet the needs of modern AI and ML systems.

2   Requirements from Existing Regulations for Perception Tasks of Train Drivers in Germany

The train driver moves a rail vehicle in various operational situations. These operational situations include the open track, the station area and shunting. Based mainly on regulations applicable to train drivers in Germany, the first seminal and complete list of perception tasks is created (Table 1). The used regulations are driving service regulation [3], DB Fernverkehr AG train driver's manual [2], as well as two rulebooks for employees in railroad operations, DBREGIO– 003 [10] and DBCDE–003 [9]. The sensor setup was evaluated on relevant use cases within these tasks and operational situations, as indicated in Fig. 1.

(a) LiDAR single ray resolution of Valeo Scala 2 (red, rotating mirror) and Ibeo NEXT (green, MEMS) for detection of fouling point indicators

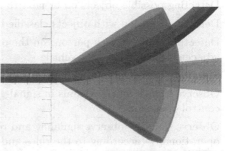

(b) DALSA Genie Nano-5GigE as front cameras with focal lengths 12 mm (red) and 75 mm (orange) shown at a minimum German railway curve radius of 180 m.

Fig. 1. Examples for considered perception tasks. Localization of fouling point indicators at railroad switches at low speeds or shunting, and object detection at high speeds for different track geometries. Indicated camera ranges denote on an estimated limit of 32 pixels per object of size 1 m for robust detection, as trainable on the CIFAR-10 [21] or ImageNet32 [7] data sets.

3   AI-Specific Requirements for Training and Testing Data

In addition to the requirements from existing regulations for train drivers as outlined in Sect. 2 and especially Table 1, training and testing data sets used in AI applications introduce additional known requirements. As an example, the AI Act [14, p.48] requires for high-risk AI systems that "Training, validation and testing data sets shall be relevant, representative, free of errors and complete. They shall have the appropriate statistical properties, [and] shall take into account, to the extent required by the intended purpose, the characteristics or elements that are particular to the specific geographical, behavioural or functional setting within which the high-risk AI system is intended to be used."

Table 1. Standard tasks and perception tasks. CC: color camera; IR-C: Infrared camera; LD: LiDAR; RD: Radar; US: Ultrasonic sensor. Checkmarks (✔) denote the applicability of a sensor to a task.

Perception tasks	Recommended sensors				
	CC	IR-C	LD	RD	US
Standard Task: Shunting train					
Compliance with the permissible speed depending on the minimum visual range	✔		✔	✔	
Continuous determination of current location	✔		✔		
Approaching a vehicle to be coupled			✔		✔
Standard Task: Observing track					
Detecting possible objects on or next to the track	✔	✔	✔	✔	
Detecting collision with objects classified as obstacles	✔	✔	✔	✔	
Detecting collision with persons on the own track or the adjacent track for another vehicle	✔	✔	✔	✔	
Standard Task: Observing railway systems					
Observe signals – fixed signals in signal-guided train control operation	✔		✔		
Observe signals – observe signaling and react accordingly operationally (according to the rules and regulations)	✔		✔		
Observe the track – detect damage and irregularities on the superstructure	✔		✔		
Observe neighboring tracks – detect damage or irregularities in oncoming trains	✔	✔	✔		
Observe neighboring tracks – detect possible obstacles in the directly neighboring tracks	✔	✔	✔	✔	
Observe catenary – detect damage and irregularities of the catenary	✔	✔	✔		
Standard Task: Controlling passenger exchange					
Monitor conditions for the door opening and closing procedure	✔	✔	✔	✔	✔
Prevent injuries to persons both between the individual vehicles in the train formation and between the vehicles and the platform edge	✔	✔	✔	✔	✔
Detect persons and objects on the platform that are at an unacceptable distance from the passenger outer doors when the doors are closed and when the train is dispatched and departing	✔	✔	✔	✔	✔
Standard Task: Observing trains					
Detect displaced load	✔		✔		

Typically, perception applications must assure that these requirements are satisfied not only with respect to the observed scene, but also with respect to the sensor characteristics. It has been noted that, for example, different scan patterns in LiDARs (Fig. 2b) inhibit the immediate transfer of models trained on one sensor to applications on another, and various approaches have been proposed to bridge this *domain gap* in practical applications [31,32], for example by means of a suitable *domain adaptation* on the data. For differences between cameras for the visible spectrum and cameras for the thermal infrared spectrum, effects and methods for domain adaptation have been proposed [6,18, e.g.]. Such techniques for domain adaption are not only employed in systems with different sensor types but also in systems using a single sensor type under different environmental conditions, e.g. modern approaches based on GANs are used to transform camera images from day to night and vice versa [19,23]. Similar techniques are used to bridge the domain gap between real and synthetic data, e.g. in case of a pose estimator [27] or in the context of stereo matching [24]. Observed effects such as accuracy losses will depend significantly on the overall AI system architecture and the intended task, in particular for deep learning-based approaches [20].

These approaches show that the domain gap is a significant problem when working with different sensor types and data under various environmental conditions, besides variations in sensor pose. In order to tackle this problem, researchers already developed various domain adaption techniques. However, these approaches are developed for specific use cases, are not validated on large data sets in the context of rail and results are often not optimal. Therefore, a huge data set covering annotated data from different sensor types is necessary to foster research in this context, providing a high variation in data along with high quality of annotations. In particular annotation efforts must be carefully considered. For instance, [8] indicates $1^1/_2$ h average *per frame* for annotation and quality control for semantic segmentation tasks (c.f. also [28] for an overview).

To achieve an ample coverage of different sensor characteristics at a minimum labeling effort, the sensor setup detailed in Sect. 4 relies on partially overlapping fields of view for heterogeneous types of sensors within the same class. Thus, a single labeling task for a given data set will provide annotated data for highly different sensor types, and thereby allow for cross-validation of methods, direct performance comparisons and bases for developing studies on domain gaps and domain adaptation.

The following sections will briefly outline the design characteristics that were primarily considered with respect to their effect on AI applications, and motivate which characteristics were determined to warrant the introduction of a dedicated sensor. Due to the availability of various sensor types and limited space, we focus on two sensor types that play a major role enabling an automation of train operations with respect to the identified standard and perception tasks listed in Table 1, i.e. camera and LiDAR sensors.

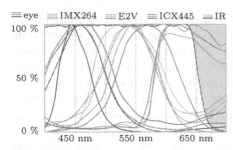

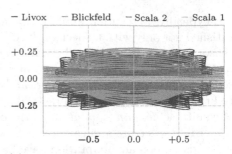

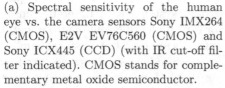

(a) Spectral sensitivity of the human eye vs. the camera sensors Sony IMX264 (CMOS), E2V EV76C560 (CMOS) and Sony ICX445 (CCD) (with IR cut-off filter indicated). CMOS stands for complementary metal oxide semiconductor.

(b) Various beam steering patterns for automotive LiDAR sensors projected onto a normalized pinhole camera plane: Livox HAP, Blickfeld Cube, Valeo Scala 2 and Valeo Scala 1.

Fig. 2. Examples of domain variations: Differences in spectral sensitivity in RGB camera sensors (a) and beam steering patterns in LiDAR sensors (b).

3.1 Camera

Resolution. While the resolution of a camera has an obvious impact on perception, lower resolutions can be computed from higher resolutions with good accuracy. Hence, the setup proposed to integrate high resolution cameras only. The evaluation determined that a 4K camera system with appropriate lens could achieve sufficient resolution to pass the vision test of human train operators according to the framework directive "DB-Rahmenrichtlinie 107.0000A02" [11] for regular operation. This was taken as an estimate for the finest required resolution.

Dynamic Range and Bit Depth. Similar to resolution, a high dynamic range and a high bit depth (providing better intensity resolution) can be used as a basis for generating lower dynamic range images. Hence, better specifications were selected for dynamic range instead of a bandwidth of different dynamic ranges. Bit depths between 8 and 24 bits per grayscale value were evaluated.

Wavelength. Differences in sensitivity to light wavelengths affect image features in various degrees. For high differences, namely between visible RGB and thermal long-wave infrared (LWIR), entirely new artefacts arise that generally require domain adaptation or retraining. Due to these differences in sensitivity and the possibility to perceive different features of the scene, the proposed specification includes visible RGB as well as LWIR cameras. Since sensitivity variations among different RGB sensors were considered minor in comparison (Fig. 2a), the choice of one type for all RGB sensors is proposed.

Rolling Shutter vs. Global Shutter. The rolling shutter effect arises in a common form of CMOS sensors, especially in consumer cameras, that read pixel lines sequentially from the camera chip to save bandwidth, leading to an offset in exposure time between image lines. The delay between first and last line of an image can exceed the exposure time by orders of magnitude. This effect can cause distinct geometrical deformations in highly dynamic scenes or under strong vibrations. For this reason, rolling shutter cameras are typically avoided in dynamic computer vision tasks (cf. [4,17]). Thus, it would be advisable to adopt global shutter cameras exclusively, which expose every pixel simultaneously.

Chip Technology. Camera chips usually use either CCD (charge-coupled device) or active-pixel sensors, commonly referred to as CMOS. Differences in appearance of the images are usually small compared to variations in chip models and camera optics. Exceptions include for example *streak* artifacts near saturated CCD image pixels, or the rolling shutter effect in some CMOS sensors. Since CMOS has almost entirely superseded CCD technology on the market and offers high resolution imaging, only CMOS sensors are recommended in the setup.

Sensor Size. The size of a camera chip affects the amount of light that falls on the area (and each pixel). This has a direct effect on image quality as smaller sensors' images are more noisy compared to larger sensors' images, especially under low light conditions. Thus, larger sensors feature a better image quality. However, larger sensors are typically more expensive and imply a larger installation space. Sensor sizes considered in the evaluation ranged from 1/2" to APS-C.

Shutter Speed and Aperture. The choice of shutter speed and aperture primarily affect the brightness of the image, and secondarily introduce motion blur and defocus that adversely affect processing. Cameras are recommended that provide an interface for manual exposure control with fast shutter speeds, e.g. for extending the dynamic range by exposure bracketing. The aperture, in contrast, is typically not modified frequently, as this (in contrast to the shutter) still requires mechanical action. Fixed-focus and fixed-aperture cameras focused at the hyperfocal distance, thereby maximizing sharpness, are recommended.

Lens. The lens in a camera can introduce distortions and chromatic aberrations that degrade image quality. They can be removed in post-processing or added synthetically with good accuracy. For this reason, it is recommended to integrate high-quality optics to provide an ideal basis for research and labeling, and degrade the quality synthetically to generate training or testing data for more economic camera/lens combinations where needed.

3.2   LiDAR

Beam Steering and Resolution. Different methods for beam steering of LiDAR sensors are currently available on the market, which lead to different scan patterns and a different ordering of acquisition time of the points (Fig. 2b). In classical rotating and rotating mirror scanners, beams follow circular patterns with a regular angle spacing. For MEMS scanners, the beam is steered by displacements of micro-scanning mirrors and can be set to follow variable vibration patterns. Scanners by the Livox company steer the beams through a pair of rotating prisms leading to a highly complex pattern. Flash scanners such as the Continental High Resolution 3D Flash LiDAR illuminate the scene simultaneously and measure the echos in a regular pixel pattern. Depending on the processing application, these differences may have a significant impact beyond performace values such as field of view, resolution or scan rate. For example, clustering algorithms such as DBSCAN [13] are dependent on accelerated queries for nearby points in large clouds. For irregular patterns, efficient queries are more difficult to define and potentially still more costly to compute. Similarly, a highly inhomogeneous spatial resolution may adversely affect approaches based on local neighborhood features, such as CNNs. To provide a basis for research in these effects, a combination of different beam steering methods is recommended. Resolutions considered in the evaluation ranged from 0,94 horizontally and 1,88 vertically down to 0,03 in either direction. Fields of view ranged from 18 to 360 horizontally, and from 5.6 to 90 vertically. Some scan patterns of proposed sensors are given in Fig. 2b.

Measurement Principle. The established measurement principle in LiDAR sensors is time of flight (ToF) measurement, where the time difference between a pulse emission and the return echo is used to determine the distance of the target. Recently, Aeva Technologies, Inc. has presented a sensor that is based on the frequency-modulated continuous wave (FMCW) principle [1]. This principle is common in radar sensors; a modulated signal is emitted, and any Doppler shift on the echo indicates a relative motion by the target. This allows to detect the motion of the sensor relative to its environment, and speeds of other objects relative to either the sensor or the environment, and can facilitate detection and tracking of moving obstacles. The specification proposes the use of both ToF scanners, due to their widespread use and type variation, as well as an FMCW scanner to explore the potentials of this new principle in comparison.

Wavelength. LiDAR sensors typically operate at wavelengths between 800 nm and 1600 nm in the near infrared domain (with longer wavelengths increasing eye safety and thus allowable power). This range is wider than the visible spectrum, hence differences in reflectance and transmission in objects are comparable to visible color differences. This can affect detection methods that utilize the echo intensity, which is provided by most state-of-the-art LiDAR sensors. More importantly, to install LiDAR sensors with overlapping fields of view, it is necessary to consider interference. Different scanners with a wide margin between operating wavelengths are less likely to interfere with each other. Wavelengths between 850 nm and 1550 nm were considered in variants of the specification.

Scan Rate. Scan rate affects recorded data in several ways. As with cameras, lower *frame* rates (i.e. the time between complete scans) can be simulated by dropping frames from higher frame rates. However, since most of the currently available scanners record the points sequentially (with the exception of flash scanners), the different recording time of points within the same scan can lead to relevant effects similar to the rolling shutter effect described for cameras (Sect. 3.1) for highly dynamic scenes. Scan rates between 10 Hz and 30 Hz were considered in the evaluation.

4   Specification of a Sensor System for ATO Research

The proposed measurement system is based, among other types, on optical, acoustic and ToF sensors, which are intended to enable an assessment of the train's state and environment. These sensors were positioned on the front, roof, sides, chassis and in the cabin of a locomotive-hauled train. A first version of the described measurement system was developed, and later discussed and refined by means of a sector survey. Figure 3 shows the resulting measurement system.

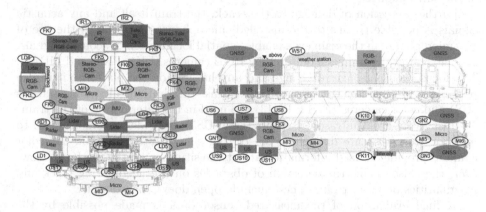

Fig. 3. Front, side and roof view of the measurement system

Ultrasonic sensors (US1–US5) are used to monitor the space immediately in front of the locomotive for obstacles or people when the train is moving slowly (e.g., shunting) and can be used to determine the distance during coupling.

The long range radar (RD2) and long range LiDAR (LD3) monitor the track ahead. The sensors focus on obstacle detection of possible objects in front of the vehicle and distance determination (e.g. to a buffer stop). In addition, short range radars (RD1; RD3) and short range LiDARs (LD1; LD5) are used to monitor the frontal area, but the main task of these systems is the lateral areas of the track. Furthermore, the area ahead is monitored by four RGB color cameras (FK5–FK8) in the upper area of the locomotive, with different fields of view. These can be used individually or combined to stereo pairs. In the latter case, depth information can be obtained. Furthermore, a supporting inspection of the overhead lines is made possible, which, however, is actually the focus of the color camera (D37) on the vehicle roof.

The detection of heat signatures (e.g. humans or animals) is performed by two LWIR cameras (IR1; IR2). They are used to detect other vehicles and obstacles during shunting, people next to the tracks, as well as irregularities and imminent dangers on the neighboring track (humans) or at the edge of the track (e.g. fallen trees). The RGB cameras (FK2; FK3) are intended to assist in these tasks and are also mounted on the locomotive with lateral orientation. Furthermore, they can be used for the detection of irregularities on oncoming trains.

The inertial measurement unit (IMU) (IM1) can be used to improve self-localization (GNSS, ETCS balises, wheel impulse generator) and detect damage to the infrastructure. Three GNSS antennas (GN1–GN3) are positioned on the vehicle roof at a large baselines in between and as far as possible clear of shadows; the three GNSS antennas are further used to detect rotational movements (roll, pitch, yaw) around the spatial vehicle axes. Additional localization support is provided by an RGB camera (FK9), enabling the detection of landmarks (e.g., church spires). In addition, the latter sensors result in an extended observation of the surroundings.

Further detection of damage to the track, the train itself and any acoustic signals is possible thanks to the installed microphones (MI1; MI2); the use of two microphones in the train even enables spatial localization of acoustic signals.

The rear of the train is monitored by RGB cameras (FK1; FK4) and LiDAR. The focus is on passenger exchange and any hazards on the platform; it is also possible to detect damage to oncoming trains. In addition, ultrasonic sensors (US) and color cameras (FK12; FK13) are used in the lateral area of the train.

Just as the front ultrasonic sensors (US1–US5), the side sensors are used to monitor areas that are difficult to see during shunting. In addition, the color cameras provide detailed information about the situation on the platform. However, they also enable the detection of obstacles on the neighboring track and irregularities on other trains. These include open doors, for example.

A final evaluation of the measured sensor data is made possible by the weather station (WS1), which collects information about the environmental conditions (temperatures, pressures, humidity) and thus enables a classification of the sensor data. There was also a passenger car under consideration with a focus on the passenger transfer [22].

5   Conclusion

The sensor setup outlined in Sect. 4 (and fully defined in [22]) covers all standard tasks with respect to their perception tasks described in Sect. 2 and listed in Table 1. Each perception task is covered by at least two different sensor types, and where suitable, different sensor variants are specified with pairwise partially overlapping fields of view, to enable studies on the impact of sensor characteristics on AI methods and to facilitate annotations benefiting multiple sensors simultaneously.

An acquisition system consisting of a locomotive and passenger cars is planned to be implemented as per the specified sensor setup. For this, a variety of additional system parameters must be specified that are not addressed here, from synchronized and calibrated acquisition and storage of data to the implementation of a semi-automatic labeling pipeline providing standardized data formats that can be harmonized across related national and international initiatives. This is intended to provide a perspective towards a program for the systematic collection of standard data sets for ATO applications in Germany and Europe.

The authors are convinced that these steps towards generic data acquisition platforms for rail applications, as the one described in this paper, and towards developing a joint data ecosystem are necessary to satisfy the need for diverse training and validation data, and to foster and accelerate research and development in ATO functions, with a particular focus on the development and validation complex AI methods in safety-critical real-time tasks.

References

1. Aeva Becomes First FMCW 4D LiDAR on NVIDIA DRIVE Autonomous Vehicle Platform. Businesswire (2022)
2. DB Fernverkehr AG: Richtlinie 418.10 - 90 "Triebfahrzeugführerheft der DB Fernverkehr AG". DB Fernverkehr AG, Frankfurt, Version 10. Accessed 15 Dec 2019
3. DB Fernverkehr AG: Richtlinie 408.20 "Fahrdienstvorschrift - Richtlinien 408.21 - 27 und 408.48". DB Netz AG, Frankfurt, Version 4.0. Accessed 12 Dec 2021
4. Baker, S., Bennett, E., Kang, S.B., Szeliski, R.: Removing Rolling Shutter Wobble. In: IEEE CVPR, pp. 2392–2399 (2010)
5. BMDV: Autonomes Fahren im Schienenverkehr. FE-Nr. 97.370/2016 (2018)
6. Bodensteiner, C., Bullinger, S., Arens, M.: Multispectral matching using conditional generative appearance modeling. In: IEEE AVSS, pp. 1–6 (2018)
7. Chrabaszcz, P., Loshchilov, I., Hutter, F.: A downsampled variant of imagenet as an alternative to the cifar datasets. arXiv:1707.08819 (2017)
8. Cordts, M., et al.: The Cityscapes dataset for semantic urban scene understanding. In: IEEE CVPR (2016)
9. DB Cargo AG, Mainz: DBCDE-003 "Regelbuch - Basisteil für Mitarbeiter im Bahnbetrieb (inkl. Führen von Triebfahrzeugen)". DB Cargo AG, Mainz, Version 04. Accessed 15 Dec 2019
10. DB Regio AG: DBREGIO-003 "Regelbuch - Basisteil für Mitarbeiter im Bahnbetrieb (inkl. Führen von Triebfahrzeugen)". DB Regio AG, Frankfurt, Version 04a. Accessed 13 Dec 2020
11. Deutsche Bahn AG: Rahmenrichtlinie 107.0000A02 Ärztliche Regeln: Med. Kriterien 5.0. In: Rahmenrichtlinie 107.0000 Grundlagen: Medizinische und psychologische Eignung 8.0 (2020)
12. Digitale Schiene Deutschland: Sensors4rail testet erstmals sensorbasierte Wahrnehmungssysteme im Bahnbetrieb (2021). https://digitale-schiene-deutschland.de/Sensors4Rail
13. Ester, M., Kriegel, H.P., Sander, J., Xu, X., et al.: A density-based algorithm for discovering clusters in large spatial databases with noise. In: KDD, pp. 226–231 (1996)
14. European Commission: Proposal for a Regulation of the European Parliament and of the Council Laying Down Harmonised Rules on Artificial Intelligence (Artificial Intelligence Act) and Amending Certain Union Legislative Acts (2021)
15. Geiger, A., Lenz, P., Urtasun, R.: Are we ready for autonomous driving? The kitti vision benchmark suite. In: CVPR (2012)

16. Harb, J., Rébéna, N., Chosidow, R., Roblin, G., Potarusov, R., Hajri, H.: FRSign: a large-scale traffic light dataset for autonomous trains. arXiv:2002.05665 (2020)
17. Hedborg, J., Forssén, P.E., Felsberg, M., Ringaby, E.: Rolling shutter bundle adjustment. In: IEEE CVPR, pp. 1434–1441 (2012)
18. Herrmann, C., Ruf, M., Beyerer, J.: CNN-based thermal infrared person detection by domain adaptation. In: Autonomous Systems: Sensors, Vehicles, Security, and the Internet of Everything, vol. 10643, p. 1064308. SPIE (2018)
19. Ho, N., Pham, M., Vo, N.D., Nguyen, K.: Vehicle detection at night time. In: NAFOSTED NICS, pp. 250–255 (2020)
20. Kalb, T., Roschani, M., Ruf, M., Beyerer, J.: Continual learning for class-and domain-incremental semantic segmentation. In: 2021 IEEE IV, pp. 1345–1351 (2021)
21. Krizhevsky, A.: Learning multiple layers of features from tiny images. Technical report (2009)
22. Leinhos, D., et al.: Sensorik als technische Voraussetzung für ATO-Funktionen. Technical report Deutsches Zentrum für Schienenverkehrsforschung (2022)
23. Lin, C.T., Huang, S.W., Wu, Y.Y., Lai, S.H.: GAN-Based Day-to-Night Image Style Transfer for Nighttime Vehicle Detection. IEEE Trans. Intell. Transp. Syst. **22**(2), 951–963 (2021)
24. Liu, R., Yang, C., Sun, W., Wang, X., Li, H.: StereoGAN: bridging synthetic-to-real domain gap by joint optimization of domain translation and stereo matching. In: IEEE/CVF CVPR, pp. 12754–12763 (2020)
25. Pappaterra, M.J., Flammini, F., Vittorini, V., Bešinović, N.: A systematic review of artificial intelligence public datasets for railway applications. Infrastructures **6**(10), 136 (2021)
26. Ristić-Durrant, D., Franke, M., Michels, K.: A Review of Vision-Based On-Board Obstacle Detection and Distance Estimation in Railways. Sensors **21**(10), 3452 (2021)
27. Rojtberg, P., Pöllabauer, T., Kuijper, A.: Style-transfer GANs for bridging the domain gap in synthetic pose estimator training. In: IEEE AIVR, pp. 188–195 (2020)
28. Sorokin, A., Forsyth, D.: Utility data annotation with Amazon Mechanical Turk. In: IEEE CVPR, pp. 1–8 (2008)
29. Tagiew, R., Buder, T., Hofmann, K., Klotz, C., Tilly, R.: Towards nucleation of GoA3+ approval process. In: HPCCT, pp. 41–47 (2021)
30. Tagiew, R., Buder, T., Tilly, R., Hofmann, K., Klotz, C.: Datensätze für das autonome Fahren als Grundlage für GoA3+. ETR - Eisenbahntechnische Rundschau 9 (2021). https://eurailpress-archiv.de/SingleView.aspx?show=2760103
31. Triess, L.T., Dreissig, M., Rist, C.B., Zöllner, J.M.: A survey on deep domain adaptation for lidar perception. In: IEEE IV Workshops, pp. 350–357. IEEE (2021)
32. Wei, Y., Wei, Z., Rao, Y., Li, J., Zhou, J., Lu, J.: LiDAR distillation: bridging the beam-induced domain Gap for 3D object detection. arXiv:2203.14956 (2022)
33. Yu, F., et al.: BDD100K: a diverse driving dataset for heterogeneous multitask learning. In: IEEE/CVF CVPR, pp. 2636–2645 (2020)
34. Zendel, O., Murschitz, M., Zeilinger, M., Steininger, D., Abbasi, S., Beleznai, C.: Railsem19: a dataset for semantic rail scene understanding. In: IEEE/CVF CVPR (2019)

Author Index

Printed in the United States
by Baker & Taylor Publisher Services